To Rolfe and Dave
Godshalk

from

Ken & Marcia Krneger

2008

You will do well to pay attention
[to the prophetic word] . . . until the day dawns
and the morning star rises in your hearts.

2 Peter 1:19 NIV

Leighton Ford

The Attentive Life

Discerning God's Presence in All Things

IVP Books

An imprint of InterVarsity Press
Downers Grove, Illinois

InterVarsity Press
P.O. Box 1400, Downers Grove, IL 60515-1426
World Wide Web: www.ivpress.com
E-mail: email@ivpress.com

InterVarsity Press® is the book-publishing division of InterVarsity Christian Fellowship/USA®, a student movement active on campus at hundreds of universities, colleges and schools of nursing in the United States of America, and a member movement of the International Fellowship of Evangelical Students. For information about local and regional activities, write Public Relations Dept., InterVarsity Christian Fellowship/USA, 6400 Schroeder Rd., P.O. Box 7895, Madison, WI 53707-7895, or visit the IVCF website at <www.intervarsity.org>.

Scripture quotations, unless otherwise noted, are from the New Revised Standard Version of the Bible, copyright 1989 by the Division of Christian Education of the National Council of the Churches of Christ in the USA. Used by permission. All rights reserved.

See p. 227 for permission credits.

Every effort has been made to trace and contact copyright holders for the materials quoted in this book. The author will be happy to rectify any omissions in future editions if notified by the copyright holders.

Design: Cindy Kiple

Images: bird: Linda Bucklin/iStockphoto
window: Ekaterina Fribus/iStockphoto

ISBN 978-0-8308-3516-4

Printed in Canada ∞

Library of Congress Cataloging-in-Publication Data

Ford, Leighton,
    The attentive life: discerning God's presence in all things/
Leighton Ford.
        p. cm.
    Includes bibliographical references (p.   ).
    ISBN 978-0-8308-3516-4 (cloth: alk. paper)
    1. God—Omnipresence. 2. Spiritual life—Christianity. 3.
    Prayer—Christianity. I. Title.
    BT132.F67 2008
    231.7—dc22

                                                                    2008002184

P	22	21	20	19	18	17	16	15	14	13	12	11	10	9	8	7	6	5	4	3	2	1
Y	26	25	24	23	22	21	20	19	18	17	16	15	14	13	12	11	10	09	08

To Jeanie

who pays attention

to God, to others, to our family

and to me

so well and so naturally

Contents

An Introduction
Short Flights and Quick Returns

I am sitting on a bench at Lost Lagoon, on the edge of the hundreds and hundreds of acres of trees and trails that make up the vast Stanley Park in Vancouver, Canada. Behind me are the tall buildings of the city. Surrounding the park on three sides are the waters of English Bay and Burrard Inlet. In the background, clouds hover over the mountains that slope down to frame Vancouver — my favorite city in the world, at least to visit.

For much of the past decade and a half I have been coming here for a summertime pilgrimage. I call it a pilgrimage not because Vancouver is such a holy place but because I can get away from my usual routines and hopefully resharpen my attentiveness and imagination.

It is a lazy midsummer afternoon, and I am alone on my spectator's perch except for a few ducks in the grass by the water's edge and some bicycle riders on the path behind me. Around the lagoon several couples are walking hand in hand.

My eye is drawn to the fountain spouting up in the center of the lagoon; from there a flight of birds take off in a perfect V-formation. They disappear, then in a few minutes come circling back, and still in formation splash down, their legs extended like the landing gears of the seaplanes descending at nearby Coal Harbor.

Hmm, I think, *short flights and quick returns*.

As I watch their landing and muse on its symbolism, a seagull comes and sits just by my foot for a minute or two as if to say: "Pay attention now. This show is for you to notice." It is a message from the birds.

Watching these birds take off and land takes my thoughts back
to when we began a new ministry of spiritual mentoring for young
leaders. At our very first board meeting the chairman asked me a
penetrating question: "What can *you* do that is unique?" His second was even more pointed: "Do you think you are doing something significant *only* when — or *mostly* when — you are traveling,
going someplace?"

His question went straight to my heart. Whether short flights or
longer ones, much of my life has been spent in going to more than
forty countries in ministry as an evangelist and preacher or on special assignment. Now that is changing. I realize that life for me will
mean not always being on the go. There will be — like the flight of
the birds — more short flights and quick returns.

My work has largely focused on evangelism — "making friends
for God," as I like to put it. But a shift has taken place. Not from
evangelism, for I am and always want to be one who shares the
good news of Jesus Christ. But now is a time to pay more attention
to my own heart, to deepen my own friendship with God and to
walk with others who want to do the same.

Vancouver itself has been one of the "busy" places I have flown
to across the years, as I have preached here in citywide meetings,
led a mission at the university, taught seminars for young leaders.
So it is fitting that around the time of my first sabbatical summer
here, *attentiveness* was beginning to matter to me. Here I discovered a new interest in drawing and painting — in learning to pay attention to what is around me.

At the same time I was trying to pay attention in new ways to
what is inside me. I read Annie Dillard's *Pilgrim at Tinker Creek*
and was struck by the way she stalked the fish in a stream near her
house in the Virginia countryside. She described how she learned
to watch for fish from an oblique angle, where her shadow would

not make them shy away. The phrase "stalking my soul" came to me then and has stuck in my imagination.

"We shall not cease from exploration." This could be a companion word from T. S. Eliot about such stalking, and those words stay with me too. It has been fascinating through the years to explore many parts of the world. Now there is still exploration to be done, and one of the reasons I have written this book and want to share it with you is that we should all be explorers, always, in all things.

LONGING AND LOOKING

Each of us is part of a Greater Story, and behind our stories is a Storyteller calling us home. The deepest longing I have is to come home to my own heart, so in a sense I am writing this book for myself. But it is not just about me, for I believe all our stories are of longing and of looking.

That has become very clear to me as I reread the notes and journals I have written in recent years. For many years "journey" was a call to go as I traveled the world in ministry. "Home" was an equally powerful inner voice calling me to stay, to be rooted. Now I realize that these were not only two ways I spent my time but also a response to two notes in my own song: the lure of the road and the call to home.

The call was to be "home on the road," to bring my real self before the real God, to be changed into his true image, to become all that God has made me to be. It was and is a longing to belong, to have a home for God in my heart.

This sense of longing runs like an underground river through the writings of many observers of the human condition, like the novelist Walker Percy. A character in his *Love in the Ruins,* the lapsed Catholic psychiatrist Tom More, sits in a sand trap on a golf course and muses, "The sand trap and the clouds put me in mind of

being ten years old and in love and full of longing. The first thing a
man remembers is longing and the last thing he is conscious of before death is exactly the same longing. I have never seen a man die
who did not die in longing."

Yet why do I so often hide from this longing? Spiritual inattentiveness, I believe, comes in large part from our fear of being
known for who we really are. Often we keep ourselves busy and
distracted because we fear that if we slow down and are still, we
may look inside and find nothing there.

If the first part of my own journey involved *longing*, the second
has encompassed mainly *looking*—coming to terms with important
parts of my soul, bringing my real self before the real God, and discovering prayer, as Simone Weil put it, as "absolute attention."

This book is about attentiveness, not simply as a path to self-
fulfillment but as the very essence of our journey to the Center—
as the way home to our own heart, the way of making our heart a
home for God. So I am writing for myself, to identify waymarks for
my own second journey but also for others who are walking the
path with Christ, or searching for the path to Christ, so we may
walk it together.

I have noticed in my own experience how the vocational journey
and the personal journey intertwine. What God is doing in both is
similar, very much like the interweaving of the intricate strands in a
Celtic cord, a work of art designed to show how God is at work
weaving the inner and outer parts of our lives into a unified pattern.

In this "second journey" I have sensed a strong call to be an artist of the soul and a friend on the journey, especially to younger
men and women, and others, who seek to be led by Jesus, to lead
like him and to lead to him, and who have a hunger to be whole
people.

Each of us is called to a life patterned by Christ. A life not shaped by inner compulsions, or captive to outer expectations, but drawn by the inner voice of love. To listen to this voice, we need to pay careful attention to where our inner and outer selves disconnect and where they need to come together in a beautiful pattern that reflects Jesus, whose inner life with his Father and outer life of ministering to others were very much one.

To walk this path home, and to be a companion to others on the journey, I need to learn both to be still and to go (or grow) deeper. T. S. Eliot wrote that "old men ought to be explorers. . . . We must be still and be moving." I do not feel old yet! But I do realize that this life stage requires not so much *doing for God* as *paying attention to what God is doing.*

There are periods in which we are mostly active and outwardly focused. And there are times in which we become more reflective, when we move more from action to being acted upon. The latter time may well come as we get older. But this is not a book about aging; it is about learning how we may become more attuned to the still, small voice of God in all the seasons of our lives.

WHAT WILL WE PAY ATTENTION TO?

In the rest of this book we will explore together various aspects of attentiveness as a special lens through which to look at our lives.

We will look at attentiveness itself: what is it, and why is it important?

We will see God as the Great Attender, the One who pays attention and call us to attention.

We will look at the *hours* of our lives, whether the hours of our days (marked by the classical "prayer hours") or the various seasons of life and our spiritual journey, and the kind of attentiveness that each phase calls for:

• the "morning" journey, when our day starts and where our life begins with all its potential and challenges

- the "midday" journey, when we are flung headlong into the busyness of life, which lures us onto the open road but may also engender a sense of having lost our way

- the "afternoon" time, when we set out in earnest on an inner journey because we know we have limited time and are heading for home

- the "evening" journey, the conscious transition from afternoon to the time when the shadows lengthen and evening falls, the time to find a way to live with a quieted soul

- the "nighttime" journey, when by God's grace all will be completed and we see darkness not as the terror of the unknown but as time to return to the great Mystery from which we set out, the final rest of our soul in God

In each chapter we will consider "one who paid attention," discovering journeyers from centuries past and our own time who have learned to pay attention and can inspire us by their examples. And in the "Practicing Attentiveness" sections we will note some of the helpful practices that from ancient times and still today have helped pilgrims to pay attention.

The appendix includes a sampling of some of the prayers I have used, a collection to help me "recollect" God's presence at the various hours of a day.

For me, discovering these new practices has not meant in the slightest jettisoning either the foundational beliefs or the spiritual disciplines that I have followed since my youth. It has meant exploring other ways: silence, stillness, art and poetry, reading Scripture not by going through great chunks but by meditating on smaller portions, listening carefully to God and my own heart, having a trusted spiritual companion as a friend on the journey.

This book is not meant to be a memoir, but it does come out of my calling to be an artist of the soul and a friend on the journey. As I seek to describe my own journey, I pray that I may be a friend traveling with you on the journey to the Friend.

There is one more thing to say: Paying attention is not a way by which we make something happen but a way to see what is already given to us. I have just reread Annie Dillard's account of stalking the fish in Virginia. She reflects both on the ancient fish symbol *(ichthus)* which stands for Christ and the way in which Mediterranean people in his day depended on finding fish in order to live. "To say that holiness is a fish is a statement of the abundance of grace; it is the equivalent of saying in a materialistic culture that money does indeed grow on trees. 'Not as the world gives do I give to you'; these fish are spirit food. And revelation is a study in stalking."

I need very much to learn to pay attention. But it is not my perfect attention that brings grace. Grace opens my eyes as I wait so that I may see both Giver and gift, and be grateful.

Often during a recent Lent I prayed a prayer that our pastor suggested: "Lord, show me what I am missing." Let us start this journey together where we are, with that prayer, and see what he shows us.

One Who Paid Attention
C. S. Lewis Looking Along a Beam

ONE DAY C. S. LEWIS STOOD in a dark toolshed where he had gone to look for something. A broad beam of sunlight was slanting in through a crack in the top of the door. As he looked at the beam with the dust motes dancing and floating in it, the shaft of sunlight captured his full attention in the darkness.

Then he moved so that the beam was falling directly on his eye. Instantly the whole scene changed. Looking out through the opening above the door, he could see up through the green leaves moving on the trees to the blue sky beyond and, millions of miles away, the sun.

It came to him then that there are two ways of looking: looking *at* and looking *along*. "Looking along the beam, and looking at the beam," he wrote, "are very different experiences."

Just so, he realized, there are two ways of looking at life: looking at the dancing and moving events, the happenings and surroundings of each day, and looking "sideways" so to speak, "along the beam"—to see not only what is happening but why, and what it is that gives meaning to the happenings of our lives.

It seems that God has made us with the capacity to look both "at" and "along" our lives, to see what is in front of us and what is beyond us, and to find that the two are not opposed ways of seeing but belong together. It is the bad fortune of our world to have separated the two, ever since the philosopher René Descartes posed a divide between mind and matter. His dualism has bedeviled us ever since. Many of us now assume that knowledge is either "scientific" and based on facts or "mystical" and based on fancy, and never the twain shall meet.

In contrast, C. S. Lewis says that Christianity is "the most materialistic" of all religions and that God must love material things: after all, he made them! We need again to heed his wisdom. True knowledge is found in the Word who became flesh, as we look both "at" and "along" the beams each and every day.

I hope that this book will help us to pay close attention both to the beams that surround us and to the Source that upholds us, in such a way that time and eternity, this world and the next, are always intersecting.

This knowledge from God and of God, and not just the experiments of the scientist or the intuitions of the mystic, will save us and transform our world.

Paying Attention
The Hours of Our Lives

Matins, lauds, prime, terce, sext, none, vespers,
compline — that your hours will pierce me with
arrows and wounds of praise.
LUCI SHAW

Time is not our enemy, nor is it a hostile place
from which we must flee.
It is a meeting place, a point of rendezvous with God.
DOROTHY BASS, RECEIVING THE DAY

Seven times a day do I praise you.
PSALM 119:164

Long centuries ago a young poet recorded praise to God that rose up in his heart seven times a day. We can surmise that he was young, because the very long psalm he wrote (the longest of all the psalms) records the longing of a young man to keep his way pure by paying attention to the words of God.

Could it be that this young poet, like David the shepherd boy, was an outdoorsman — or possibly even David himself? If so we may imagine that he was accustomed to tell the time of day by observing the angle of the sun, and evening time by the rising of the moon.

In those long-ago days, time was measured by positions of the heavenly bodies, not by mechanical devices. The young poet marked the segments of his days by the seven times he stopped to lift praise to the Creator, whom he knew as the God who separated light from darkness, who called the light Day and the darkness Night.

This poet may have been one of the very first of our human race to observe specific hours of the day as times to lift up his heart in prayer: surely at dawn and midday and sunset, at the times he gave thanks for his food, and perhaps when he rose at night. Others whose stories are told in the Bible followed this example with their own set hours of prayer; Daniel, for example, knelt down three times a day to give thanks to God (Dan 6:10).

So "the hours" early became reminders to pay attention to God.

THE BENEDICTINE HOURS

Centuries passed, and another young man began looking for a way to order his life toward God. Born in Italy in A.D. 480 to a noble Roman family, he was a student in Rome in his late teens when he became dismayed by the dissolute lives of his fellow students and gave up the wealth of his father's house, desiring only to serve God.

Leaving Rome, he settled in a hill village about forty miles away and became part of a community of men who shared his view of life. Then for three years he lived as a hermit, alone in a cave by a lake, where it was reported that he was fed by ravens.

At last an abbot, impressed by his devotion, asked him to lead a nearby community. There this young man became a shepherd of souls, founded a monastery that became the center of his life's work, and eventually became known as St. Benedict. He wrote a "rule of life," a guideline we choose to regulate our lives in order to facilitate our spiritual growth. Benedict's rule could be summed up in three words: "Pray and work." The Benedictine Rule included his own version of "the hours."

The hours were not a ritual to be mechanically observed. They were meant to be an attentive path leading to new vision. "Apertis oculis nostris," Benedict said at the start of the Rule. "Let us open our eyes."

Benedict's prayer hours began with Lauds in the morning and carried through Compline at the end of the day. His cycle became the widespread practice of the church through the centuries, a tradition that is carried on today especially in religious orders and communities and by clergy as part of public worship services.

My first experience of the hours came during a retreat at Mepkin Abbey, a lovely monastery in the low country of South Carolina. Growing up in the Protestant evangelical tradition, for many years before that I had been unaware of the hours. In more liturgically aware churches, on the other hand, the hours have sometimes been regarded as the obligation of the clergy and not for ordinary people. In fact Benedict wrote his Rule for laypeople, not clerics! His original purpose was not to organize an order of clerics but to provide a guide for ordinary laypeople who wanted a lifestyle of following Christ day to day.

While religious orders around the world observe these specified

THE DIVINE HOURS

The "divine hours" as traditionally practiced by religious orders usually include the following:

- **Vigils, about 3 a.m.**

- **Lauds, greeting the beginning of the day**

- **Prime, the start of the day's work**

- **Terce, the third hour, perhaps midmorning**

- **Sext, midday**

- **None, midafternoon**

- **Vespers, as the day is over and evening comes**

- **Compline, when the day is complete and sleep begins**

hours of prayer, originally they were meant to call all Christian believers to pay attention to God throughout their days—as was the
case with the well-known Angelus at noontime. In the late Middle
Ages, when printed books became widely available in Europe,
there was a great production of beautifully illuminated manu-
scripts known as Books of Hours. Although written in Latin, they
became bestsellers and were tremendously popular as prayer
guides for the ordinary everyday people.

AN INVITATION TO PRACTICE THE HOURS

Observing the hours can be a helpful practice for us in learning
to pay attention to God throughout our days. Further, the hours
can also be an illuminating way to reflect on the seasons or passages of our lives. I invite you to explore with me as we pay attention to how God has been and is at work in each of the "hours"
we have lived.

Our word *hour* goes back to the Greek word *hora*, which, David
Steindl-Rast points out, originally meant more than a unit of time.
It was "not a numerical measure," he writes, "but a soul measure."
Isn't it true that we usually think of the seasons of the year less in
terms of the dates they begin and end than in terms of their effect
on us: the cold of winter, the awakening of spring, the glow of summer, the pathos of autumn leaves falling? All these seasons speak
deeply to our inner life. Just so we may think of hours as seasons
of our life—the passages of our soul.

The most vital way to measure our lives is not by chronological
time—*chronos* time, to use the Greek word—but in terms of
kairos, the word often used in the Bible to speak of those oppor-
tune times that become turning points. *Kairos* is the word Jesus
often used when he said, "My time is not yet," or "My time has
come." To be fully alive is to pay attention to kairos encounters. As

Paul wisely counseled his readers, "Be very careful, then, how you live—not as unwise but as wise, making the most of every opportunity because the days are evil" (Eph 5:15-16 NIV).

I like to think of the attentive life also as the *contemplative* life, for *contemplative* literally means "putting together." We connect the dots between the chronos and the kairos of our life, relate the hours that we measure by the clock to the hours and seasons of our soul.

Out of years of frustration as I tried and often failed to pay closer attention to God day to day, I have developed my own version of the hours. It is becoming a way to rein in my wandering mind and to weave together the inner and outer threads of my life. For me, observing the hours has become less a discipline to keep and more a reminder to be aware of God's presence in whatever I am doing and wherever I am. You might say it is a kind of UPS— Universal Positioning System. For a recent Christmas I even asked my son-in-law for a watch with timer and bells, which I set to remind me at certain hours to stop, remember and pray!

PAY ATTENTION

From the time we were children we were told to "pay attention," as if this were the simplest thing in the world. But in fact attentiveness is one of the most difficult concepts to grasp and one of the hardest disciplines to learn. For we are very distractible people in a very distracting world.

God wants us to be attentive people, as he is an attentive God. Many of the words of God in the Bible call his people to "look," "see," "listen," "give heed." Jesus (as paraphrased by Eugene Peterson in *The Message*) said in his Sermon on the Mount, "Give your entire attention to what God is doing right now" (Mt 6:34).

The influential French writer Simone Weil believed that attention is the very heart of prayer, and her French forebear Blaise Pascal also felt that inattention is the greatest enemy of the spiritual life. Their conviction, which is also that of many spiritual teachers through the ages, deserves our careful attention. Our world distracts us in many ways. Yet attentiveness, as I have come to see, is most critical for us to find the way to clarity of heart, and clarity is the path to seeing God, who is the source and end of all our longing.

"Blessed are the pure in heart," said Jesus—we could translate this saying as "Blessed are the clear at center"—"for they shall see God." Such is the promise for those whose hearts—their personal centers—are directed toward God.

Moses was one who paid attention. In the desert, having fled from Pharaoh's court, out tending his sheep, he saw a bush that was burning but did not burn up. "I must turn aside and look at this great sight," he said. "When the LORD saw that he had turned aside . . . God called to him" (Ex 3:3-4). That desert place became holy ground where Moses heard God's call to save his people from slavery in Egypt.

The "burning bushes" in our path are signs planted in our life, opportunities to listen and pay attention. How often does God put signs out that we miss because our life is filled with so much stuff?

Long after Moses' burning bush encounter, he was summoned with the elders of Israel to meet God on Mount Sinai. The book of Exodus contains a magnificent description of what they saw. Under God's feet appeared "something like a pavement of sapphire stone, like the very heaven for clearness" (Ex 24:10). In my inner eye I picture a clear expanse of open blue sky and imagine the greatness of God, for whom the sky, metaphorically, is a pavement on which he walks, with the clearness of heaven bringing clarity to the very rocks of the earth.

When Jesus was transfigured, that same clarity of light made his clothes blaze with a bright whiteness, brighter than any launderer could make them, as the voice of the Father told the disciples: "This is my Son, the Beloved; . . . listen to him" (Mt 17:5).

This is the clarifying light that I seek: to be "clear at center" and so with true attentiveness "to see God in all things, and all things in God."

PAYING ATTENTION TO THE OTHER

Attentiveness means respecting, attending to, waiting on, looking at and listening to the other—the persons and things that we encounter—for what they are in themselves, not what we can make of them. We are called to pay attention to the Other—our Creator God—to know and worship him.

Paradoxically, attentiveness may be just the opposite of "fixing our attention." Instead it involves a letting go of our usual need to control, an opening of ourselves to what we are being told or shown.

Our instinct is to hold on.

Elia Kazan said of the poet Sylvia Plath that "the world for Sylvia Plath only existed for her to write about." Plath paid attention to her work and her words, but the possessiveness that consumes is the opposite of the attentiveness that frees and transforms.

During one of my retreats at Mepkin Abbey, I wanted to do a watercolor painting, and after several days I selected a large spreading oak tree to serve as my subject. I spent an hour or two painting plein air. The next day as I was leaving, a regret stabbed me: I realized I had treated that tree only as an object for me to paint, had not really attended to it as a tree made by God and beautiful in itself. In a penitential mood, I turned my car, drove back to where that tree stood, and (hoping no one else was looking) walked up to the tree, put my arms as far around it as I could reach, and asked God to help me to honor the tree as valuable for what he had made it to be, not just how useful it was to me!

Sin, as Augustine defines it, is to be *incurvatus in se* — curved in on oneself. The Quaker writer Douglas Steere defined sin as inattention. "For prayer is awakeness, attention, intense inward openness. In a certain way sin could be described . . . [as] anything that destroys this attention." Salvation — true freedom — is just the opposite of sin, turning us out to the reality of the created world of which we are a part, and to the Creator who calls us to be attenders.

THE GOD WHO PAYS ATTENTION

Friends (and some not-so-friendly persons) are always e-mailing stuff that I didn't ask for and usually don't want. Most often I just hit delete. But one forwarded message insisted I pull it up. In astonishment I watched "The Powers of Ten," a series of images showing our galaxy from the most distant reaches to one of the tiniest particles of our earth.

Beginning with images of the Milky Way ten million light-years from the Earth, it moved through space in successive leaps through our solar system to the orbits of the planets Mercury, Venus, Earth, Mars, Jupiter, to our earth and the Western Hemisphere, down to the southeastern United States and to Tallahassee, Florida. At Tallahassee it zoomed in to the buildings of the National High Magnetic Field Laboratory, then to a tall oak tree, followed successively by the surface of a leaf measuring one millimeter, to one cell of the leaf at 100 nanometers, to a strip of DNA, down through the atoms that make up the leaf to a single proton, and finally ended with the tiniest particle, a quark measuring 100 atometers.

Awesome! That was the only word that came to mind. I had just seen the world from the tiniest bit out to the edge of our galaxy ten million light years off!

When our granddaughter Christine came by on her way home

from high school, I showed her the "Powers of Ten," and she was as awestruck as I was.

"Do you think we have just had a small glimpse of the way God sees things? Close up and distant, all in a moment?" I asked.

"I think so," she nodded.

Of course, if God is really there (and here), then what took the highest-powered microscopes and telescopes (and the Internet) for Christine and me to view for a moment—a reality millions of light-years old—God has had in view totally, instantly, constantly since creation itself exploded into being.

It is a mind- and heart-boggling thought, but not a new one. Centuries ago the writer of Psalm 8 (presumably David the shepherd boy who had spent many nights in the fields looking after sheep and gazing at the stars) wrote:

When I look at your heavens, the work of your fingers,
     the moon and the stars that you have established;
what are human beings that you are mindful of them,
     mortals that you care for them? (Ps 8:3-4)

Christine and I can now see our world in dimensions both tinier and huger than David could have dreamed of. But in the light of the "powers of ten"—the powers of scientific observation—perhaps the question has changed from "What are human beings that you are mindful of them?" to "If the universe is so huge, why should we think that God would pay attention to us anyway?"

Many in the generation of Christine's parents (and grandparents) assume that the picture of God as the Shepherd of our souls and of the stars is a quaint relic of a romantic worldview long ruled out by science.

The great new truth is that the perspective of science has changed. The belief that science rules out God is itself now quaint!

And Christine's peers are part of a generation seeking to know God in a deep and personal way.

THE GOD WHO ATTENDS TO US

The story of the Bible is not merely the story of a deity who launched the cosmos and then turned his attention elsewhere. Quite the contrary: it reveals a God who is mindful, who keeps paying attention, whose mind does not wander! He is a Father who watches with careful attention.

This is the very nature of God, and a truth that touches the deepest longings of our lives.

Bilquis Sheikh, a Muslim woman, was brought to faith in Christ by coming to know God as a loving Father. She describes the moment after a long search when this truth seized her imagination: "A breakthrough of hope flooded me. Suppose God were like a father? If my earthly father would put aside everything to listen to me, why wouldn't my heavenly Father do the same?"

She went to her knees and reached over to a bedside table where she kept both the Bible and the Qur'an. Lifting them, one in each hand, she prayed: " 'Which, Father? Which one is Your Book?' And then a remarkable thing happened. . . . I heard a voice inside my being, a voice . . . full of kindness, yet at the same time full of authority. And the voice said, 'In which book do you meet Me as your Father?' 'In the Bible.' That's all it took."

The Qur'an that Muslims read uses many respectful terms to speak of the greatness of God. But it has no name for God as *Father.* For the devout Muslim to associate God with human beings in an intimate and personal way is to commit the sin of "shirk"—of associating God with what is not God. Yet a friend in Cairo has told me that his Muslim friends are deeply touched when he promises to pray to God for their needs—the Father who, as Bilquis Sheikh wrote, would "put aside everything to listen to me."

THE MINDFULNESS OF GOD

This God creates, playfully, purposefully—out of nothing—space and stars, sun and moon, light and darkness, dandelions and donkeys, whales and kingfishers, and a handsome couple. And then he doesn't get bored: he *sees* everything he has made and takes delight in it. And instead of standing at a distance, he comes to visit his creatures in a garden in the cool of the evening.

But things don't go happily ever after. Still, when Adam and Eve are not mindful of him and the good boundaries he has set, he doesn't walk away and wash his hands. He walks in the spoiled garden and calls "Where are you?"—still paying attention.

Later he does wash the whole world he made with a flood. But even then he is paying attention, starting the creation all over again with one man and his family and an ark like a menagerie of animals. Not one escapes his attention!

The story goes on. He pays attention to one nomad, Abraham, and makes him a father of nations. Pays attention to the cries of slaves, and makes Moses pay attention to a burning bush so he will heed the call to lead them out.

And this God looks with *in*sight as well as sight. Why does God choose David as the king of Israel? While the people choose leaders because they look attractive on the outside, God looks on "the heart." He sees that this shepherd lad, who pays attention to stars and sheep, also knows that "the eyes of the LORD are on the righteous, and his ears are attentive to their cry" (Ps 34:15 NIV).

Fast-forward through the centuries. Wayward as his people are, God never stops paying attention, until he comes up with the biggest attention-getter of all. The lens of the story moves in from wide-angle to close-up. It zooms in on one unmarried virgin, who listens with her heart when the angel Gabriel comes to tell her that God is paying special attention to her.

And he pays attention quietly. His son is born not in a palace with fanfare and flares across the evening sky but in a manger, in the stillness of a Middle Eastern night.

We all know there is a difference between people who pay attention to us, which we all want deeply, and those who force their attentions on us, which something in us resists strongly. God pays, not demands, attention. And yet the greatest wonder of all is that when we ignore him, he still longs for, yearns for, our attention.

Jesus told the story of a landowner whose tenant farmers do not pay attention to their work or to him, who refuse to pay him what they owe. The landowner sends messengers to ask them to pay up, but they beat and shamefully treat them. Finally he sends his own son, sure they will respect this final gesture. But shamefully, they seize and kill the son.

It is more than a parable. God does send his Son to live in his own creation and to seek our attention. He pays attention without clamor—to the fine smoothness of the wood he planes in the carpenter's shop . . . to the words of God he learns from the ancient Scripture . . . to the stirrings of his own young heart sensing that he must above all be about his Father's business.

When the time comes, Jesus pays attention

- to the bronzed faces of the fishermen he calls to be with him
- to the hardened faces of the tax collectors and offbeat characters he recruits as his disciples
- to the longing face of an outcast woman by a well
- to the seeking face of a philosopher who comes to talk by night

- to the pleading face of one blind beggar by the road
- to the taunting faces of the soldiers who nail him to the cross
- to the pain-wracked face of a thief dying beside him on the cross
- to his mother, whom in his last moments he commends to the care of his beloved disciple John

He is the Great Attender!

And the mind with which he paid attention was the mind of his Father—the One who had been paying attention all along.

"Don't you know," he said (here I paraphrase), "that God pays attention to one broken-winged sparrow when it falls? That he pays attention to the flowers in springtime? That he is so detail-oriented that he can tell you exactly how many hairs are left on your balding skull?"

Once he painted a word picture of this God.

Don't you know that God is like a father whose no-account son has demanded his inheritance, left home and squandered it all on wine, women and song? But this father waits every evening at the gate of the village, peering into the distance, never for a moment forgetting that ne'er-do-well. And when the son drags himself home, broke and broken, the father sprints out to give him a huge hug, throwing for him the biggest party you ever saw, giving him a brand-new wardrobe and the finest jewelry as if he were the very best son a father could ever have. Don't you know God is like that? (see Lk 15)

"No," his amazed listeners would say, "we have no fathers like that in our village. We would either declare such a son as dead to us, no son at all, or if he came back begging, put him on probation for a long time."

To which Jesus would reply, so gently, so strongly: "But that is exactly what God is like. God loves like that. His love is focused attention. He does not force his attention on you. But he still longs for you." And out of that love Jesus himself wept over the city that had ignored him, lamenting that he had longed to gather Jerusalem's children together "as a hen gathers her chicks under her wings, but you were not willing" (Mt 23:37 NIV).

WHAT WOULD IT BE LIKE IF GOD DID NOT PAY ATTENTION?

What if he did withdraw it from us? G. K. Chesterton suggested that the sun rises over and over again because God is enjoying it so much! Suppose his mind wandered and he forgot what time it was, and sunrise and sunset did not happen?

What if God simply got bored with the banality of our evil and overlooked seedtime and harvest? Or if he got distracted with the other billions of planets and forgot when it was our time to be born? Or to die?

One night when David the shepherd king could not sleep, with the weight of his nation on his shoulders and his soul, he lay awake remembering the long nights out in the fields when he was a boy watching to protect the flocks from wolves. Perhaps that night he composed another poem and prayer about God—"the One who watches over Israel," the One who "neither slumbers nor sleeps."

But suppose God does seem to go to sleep on us? There is more than one place in the Bible where people demand him to wake up, and not too politely either.

"Rouse yourself!" rages the writer of Psalm 44, upset that God had done things for his ancestors but has been silent in his day. "Why do you sleep, O Lord? Awake, do not cast us off forever!" (Ps 44:23). Jesus' own disciples woke him from a sound sleep when their fishing boat was foundering in a squall. "Do you not care that we are perishing?" they demanded (Mk 4:38).

One of the most poignant songs I have heard in a long time is by the Rwandan folk singer Jean-Paul Samputu. His mother, father, three brothers and a sister were slaughtered in the terrible genocide that took a million lives in ninety days. Jean-Paul drowned his grief in drugs and drink for three years until the healing power of God changed his life. Now he sings songs of reconciliation and peace and beauty. But the first song he wrote after his family's murders was "God, Where Were You That Day?"—the day his family died.

Which of us could not sing that same song? I could have when our son Sandy died during surgery to correct a life-threatening heart problem. The day before his surgery, my stomach was so tied up in knots, so anxious, that I just had to get out and run. When I stopped, on a road above his college campus, I talked with God. Maybe it is better to say I argued with God. I said, "Lord, I know you can heal Sandy through this surgery if you want to. If you don't want to, I can't see why you don't. I'm his father. I would heal him if I could." Finally I said, "God, I just want to ask one thing: be good to my boy tomorrow."

Sandy did not survive. His heart was lethally wrong; our hearts were broken. Was God not paying attention as hundreds of friends around the world were praying?

There are certainly times when God does not *seem* to be paying attention. Jesus himself in his last moments cried, "My God, why? Why have you forsaken me?" Later in this book we will explore what it means to pay attention to God during those dark times when his face seems to be turned away.

For me the death of our son was one of them. Yet on the long drive home from that hospital my wife, Jeanie, sitting beside me with a drawn and ravaged face, said simply: "Either there is a God and he is good, or there is no God at all. It is just as stark a choice as that."

How do we make that terrible choice? Or, better, how are we

chosen? I offer no easy answers as to why God's attentions sometimes seem absent and at other times are not at all welcome. Sometimes we may almost wish he would leave us alone. As a Jewish
person reflecting on the persecutions Jews have suffered said, "I
wish God would choose someone else for a change." Some things
happen that are so horrifying they almost demand silence, and certainly cheap "answers" do no good.

Yet in part I am writing about attention because it has often been
during the darkest hours that God has gotten my attention and
taught me to pay attention. It hasn't happened quickly, and the process has often been terribly painful, like groping through a dense
fog toward a wavering and distant light. Still the light has burned
on. And I am still learning the truth of the old hymn about God who
"standeth in the shadows," keeping watch-care over his own.

There were those who held on to us at those times when our
faith was feeble—sometimes with a brief and honest word, more
often just by being present with us. I have learned that God does
not do his attending all by himself. He has set the world up so that
he has deputies—his "attendants" if you will, namely you and me.
He pays attention to us human beings so that we in turn may be the
tenders of his world.

When someone tried to compliment an old gardener on the
beauty of his well-tended garden, saying, "God and you have done
a great job," he retorted, "You should have seen it when God had
it all by himself."

Which gets to the point of the story: God pays attention and calls
us to be a people who pay attention. Like it or not, he has put us
here in his world as his gardeners, to tend it as he tends us, and as
his shepherds, to watch over his people as he watches over us.
"Feed my sheep," Jesus said to his often stumbling disciple Peter.
"Feed my sheep."

If this is so, why then the weeds in the garden? And the wolves among the sheep?

Is it because we refuse his attention, and will not pay attention?

WELCOMING GOD'S ATTENTION — OR NOT

There are people whose attentions we resent because they are very annoying. And it may be that sometimes we resent God's attentions not so much out of a reasoned denial of his existence as from a deep instinctive refusal to conform to what we perceive as some kind of celestial busybody who tries to run everyone else's affairs.

Simon Tugwell is a British scholar who has a deep understanding of how our imaginative "cramps" — our pictures of God — affect our belief, or lack of it. He remembers from his childhood an old Book of Common Prayer with a picture of Guy Fawkes trying to sneak a bomb into the Houses of Parliament. At the top of the picture was an enormous eye watching him. Here was an image of God as the "all-seeing eye, the ever-present policeman, constantly prying into our misdeeds."

The amazing thing is that the God who shows himself in Jesus does not force his attentions upon us. He knocks and waits. Jesus was described as the one who does not "wrangle or cry aloud" (Mt 12:19), and the great picture in the book of Revelation shows him knocking at the door of our heart, not battering the door down (Rev 3:21). No wonder Julian of Norwich used to call him "my courteous Lord."

Pity that we are tone-deaf to his voice and his knock. Perhaps inattentiveness is our greatest sin — not only against him but against ourselves.

We "use selective inattention and forgetting to get through life," writes Marshall Jenkins; we assume "it is the crazy pace of our lives that is killing us when really it's our inattention to our deepest desire, the desire for God."

Our inattentive selves are like the people Jesus told about who were invited to a wedding feast but were so wrapped up in their everyday concerns that they made every excuse in the world to stay away from what could have been the greatest night of their lives.

REGRETS ONLY

**For admiring the painting
and not knowing the artist
wanted to meet you.**

**For pulsing with joy
and never realizing
there was a source.**

**For tasting the sweetness
    and the savor
and not thinking to ask
who made it so good.**

**For longing for love
and not dreaming
that love was longing
    for you.**

**For remembering that an
    invitation came
and not being able to recall
what exactly you did with it.**

**For walking by an open door
and never wondering when
would be closing time.**

NEAR HARTWELL HOUSE,
AYLESBURY, ENGLAND
SEPTEMBER 30, 2003

When Paul wrote to the Christians at Rome his profound theological treatise on the human condition, he began with a powerful overture in which he says that inattentive human beings are "without excuse; for though they knew God, they did not honor him as God or give thanks to him, but they became futile in their thinking" (Rom 1:20-21). So spiritual inattentiveness leads to a kind of spiritual amnesia.

One night a large audience waited in a concert hall in Cleveland, Ohio, for a symphony performance to begin. Suddenly all were startled as a man stepped out from the wings onto the stage, shielded his eyes against the footlights, and called out, "Is there anybody here who can tell me who I am?"

In a very real sense we humans are spiritual amnesiacs, trying to remember who we are, where we came from, and where we must go to come home to our hearts.

And the God who calls us to attention is really calling us to the discovery of who we are: human beings made to pay attention — not to be "lost in the cosmos" (the title of a Walker Percy novel about human longing) but rather, as Esther De Waal has written, "to be 'lost in wonder.' "

One late afternoon I walked down a country lane in England, not far from Oxford, to the edge of a plowed field. There, watching the sun slanting and bathing the landscape in a glowing beauty, I was reminded that C. S. Lewis, the famous Oxford professor, spoke of how as a young atheist he had been "surprised by joy" — aware again and again of stabs of joy that pierced him as he read poetry and pondered beauty, joy from some unknown source, animating a longing deep within, intimating the God who was seeking him.

That evening I also remembered, with deep poignancy, Jesus' story of the invitation to the wedding feast and the guests who disregarded it, sending *regrets only.*

THE QUALITIES OF ATTENTIVENESS

Poets, writers, artists, naturalists all help us to understand what it means to "attend" and teach us that we can think of attentiveness in many ways.

Being fully present in the moment. "Simple attention to the present . . . In these moments of attention to the present, each moment stands alone and becomes a visitation, a presence in its own right."

Looking long enough. "If one looks long enough at almost anything, looks with absolute attention at a flower, a stone, the bark of a tree, grass, snow, a cloud, something like revelation takes place. Something is 'given,' and perhaps that something is always a reality outside the self."

Looking freshly at what is familiar. Harvard naturalist Louis Agassiz once said that he had spent the summer traveling. Then he added that he only got halfway across his own backyard. Similarly, one summer while recovering from a heart "attack" I did not travel but spent much of my time doing a painting of our own backyard. It has become a reminder to me that I do not need to travel to see what the poet Gerard Manley Hopkins saw: "there lives the dearest freshness deep down things."

Being available. Attentiveness means a willingness to listen for God's voice—and readiness to obey! Interestingly, as Henri Nouwen points out, our word *audio* comes from the Latin *audire*, which has the sense of "to obey" or "to heed."

Becoming aware. To live with "continuous awareness" (as the naturalist Joseph Wood Krutch put it) in each moment is an art that requires practicing. Abraham Heschel reminds us,

> The art of awareness of
>   God,
> the art of sensing His presence in our daily lives
> cannot be learned offhand.

Waiting with expectancy. Attention is closely related to the French word *attendre*, which means "to wait." Recalling that an important aspect of monastic

THRICE
(1 Samuel 3)

Samuel
Once.
Samuel
Twice.
Samuel
Thrice.

And in the dimming dusk
old eyes grown weak
lamp not yet trimmed
a pair of sleepy, boyish ears
pricked up
and thought three times
they heard
a voice
a voice they did not know
an older, newer, wiser, deeper,
bolder voice
and finally knew it was
Another Voice
and came to full attention.

Thrice
would I in my
dawning dreams
hear
that Voice
that Other Voice

Beneath the sounds that daily
clamor my attention

that Voice I know
and listen for again
prompting my older heart
let go
calling my younger soul
lead on.

life has been described as "attentive waiting," the poet/essayist Kathleen Norris comments, "I think it's also a fair description of the writing process. Once, when I was asked, 'What is the main thing a poet does?' I was inspired to answer, 'We wait.' A spark is struck; an event inscribed with a message—this is important, pay attention—and a poet scatters a few words like seeds in a notebook. Months or even years later, those words bear fruit. The process requires both discipline and commitment, and its gifts come from both preparedness and grace."

Being mindful. There is a lovely story of a monk who was very upset because he had lost his umbrella. When a brother monk asked why he was so bothered, he answered that it showed he had lost his attentiveness!

As one who forgets more often than I like to admit where I parked my car or left my glasses, I need this reminder.

Being wakeful. Jesus, telling his disciples to "watch and pray" (Mk 14:38 NIV) and not be led into temptation, and Paul, admonishing the early believers that "it is now the moment for you to wake from sleep" (Rom 13:11), emphasized the importance of wakefulness. As a Senegalese proverb puts it: "The opportunity which God sends does not wake up him who is sleeping."

Writing on prayer, C. S. Lewis recommended wakefulness as the way to penetrate God's disguises: "We may ignore, but we can nowhere evade, the presence of God. The world is crowded with

Him. He walks everywhere *incognito*. And the *incognito* is not always hard to penetrate. The real labour is to remember, to attend. In fact, to come awake. Still more to remain awake."

CAN WE LEARN TO BE ATTENTIVE?

Some people seem to be born with a special "attentiveness quotient." Great athletes are gifted in this way. Ted Williams, perhaps the greatest baseball hitter of all time, was immensely endowed with athletic vision. He allowed that hitting a baseball is the single most difficult thing to do in sports. Yet at the height of his career with the Boston Red Sox, his eyesight was so legendary that it was claimed he could see the seams on a ninety-mile-an-hour fastball! Some physicists who have studied batting pooh-pooh this, saying it is impossible. Yet one sportswriter said that trying to get a fastball past Ted Williams was "like trying to get a sunbeam past a rooster."

Take another fabled figure, the mathematician John Nash. By the age of thirty he had become a legend for his mathematical genius. Then, as Sylvia Nasar relates in her biography of Nash, *A Beautiful Mind*, he had the first shattering episode of paranoid schizophrenia. For the next three decades he suffered from delusions and hallucinations, and because of this "cancer of the mind" he was often hospitalized and unable to cope with his life or focus on his work. Yet, amazingly, years later he recovered and won a Nobel Prize and international fame.

Nash's genius in part lay in his uncanny ability to concentrate. He was "always buried in thought . . . always thinking," as a university contemporary remembers. "If he was lying on a table, it was because he was thinking. Just thinking." Yet his focus was not on reading books, and nobody seemed to remember seeing him with a book during his graduate days. Instead he quizzed others, made constant notes and thought. He was able to formulate his ground-breaking theorems because while other mathematicians could focus on a problem for days at a time, Nash could do so for months.

Clearly there are those gifted with a surpassing ability to focus. But what about the rest of us ordinary mortals?

There is no such thing for us humans as complete attentiveness. In part this is because each of us attends to different things. Our daughter Debbie, who is trained in the Myers-Briggs Type Indicator, describes a morning she spent with Jeanie and me in Florida. Having recently begun to draw and paint, I had been reading a book in which the art historian Sister Wendy Beckett reflects on abstract contemporary art and brought it to show to Jeanie and Debbie.

"Mom was totally absorbed in the alligators and the birds and the trees," she laughs, "while Dad was excited about an abstract painting in a devotional book he was reading. She was being herself—a classic Myers-Briggs S type who is aware of what is around her, while Dad was the classic N intuiting what the painting was doing inside him."

Debbie explained that the S or "sensing" individual is very aware of what is seen with one's eyes—of sensory reality and details—while the N or "intuitive" person pays attention more easily to what is "unseen"—to patterns and possibilities, insight and symbolism. So both Jeanie and I were paying attention—but to different things.

Yet while our preferences may differ, the call to all of us is to see God in all things, and all things in God. What a demanding call!

In a book on the nature of seeing, James Elkins writes,

At first, it appears that nothing could be easier than seeing. We just point our eyes where we want them to go, and gather in whatever there is to see. Nothing could be less in need of

explanation. . . . The truth is more difficult: seeing is irra-
tional, inconsistent, and undependable. . . . Our eyes are not
ours to command; they roam where they will and then tell us
they have only been where we have sent them. No matter how
hard we look, we see very little of what we look at. . . . Ultimately, seeing alters the thing that is seen and transforms the
seer. Seeing is metamorphosis, not mechanism.

Perhaps by now you are wondering: If seeing and paying attention is so complex and difficult, why bother with it? Is there not
some easier way?

Consider again Elkins's words: "Seeing alters the thing that is
seen and transforms the seer. Seeing is metamorphosis, not mechanism." These words lift my hopes. They remind me of the words
of Paul that there may be "veils" that hide us from God, yet "when
one turns to the Lord, the veil is removed. Now the Lord is the
Spirit, and where the Spirit of the Lord is, there is freedom. And
all of us, with unveiled faces, seeing the glory of the Lord as though
reflected in a mirror, are being transformed into the same image
from one degree of glory to another; for this comes from the Lord,
the Spirit" (2 Cor 3:16-18).

See! Attention is indeed metamorphosis, not mechanism; freedom, not legalism; the creation of the Lord the Spirit, not of our
own half-hearted efforts; the promise that there will be glory—for
"all of us," not just a few specially gifted spiritual masters.

STEPPING INTO ATTENTIVENESS

Is attentiveness a gift to use? an art to practice? a work to per-
form? It seems to include some of all three. But it is certainly a
call of God, and it is the call and practice that I myself hope to
awaken to, more and more, in the writing of this book.

Agnes Cunningham, a writer and teacher, discovered as a

thirteen-year-old in her first year of high school that she had an unusual ability to listen. One of her classmates had given a report
about which Agnes was assigned to write an essay. Later her English teacher summoned her to explain how she had been able to
give an almost word-for-word version of what her classmate said.
Had she copied it from her paper?

"I just listened to what she was saying" was her only response.
That led her to become aware that she did try to listen with focused
attention to most of what she heard. Where had this awareness
come from? "I do not know where or how I learned to listen in that
way. With the passage of time I have learned that the ability for
such listening is a gift to be treasured; to be mined; to be used as
the pathway to a deeper, more interior kind of listening. I have
learned what is meant when the early fathers of the church talk
about the 'ear of the heart.'"

As Cunningham came to see, attentiveness is both a gift to treasure and a discipline to practice. The attentive eye and ear come
from "the attentive heart . . . a new heart, a simple heart, a pure
heart . . . a heart given by God."

But the gift must be nurtured through the spiritual discipline of
discernment, a continual kind of "eye-washing" in which we welcome the things that bring transparency and avoid those things
that dull our vision. "Discernment," Cunningham writes, "is
needed so that the attentive heart can be about its one purpose: to
lead the disciple to live so as to begin to know, even now, a foretaste
of what the human heart has not yet conceived."

That leads me to one final definition: love is focused attention.
We will explore that more together. But for now let that thought
draw us on: that the God who is Love is giving his focused attention
to us. And that is why the path of attentiveness is worth pursuing.

The power of attentiveness to connect was illustrated for me at a dinner with friends, one of whom is the director of a large medical center. Michael told of us of a spiritual journey he made to the Middle East with a group of men. One day the leader took them into a remote area and told each of them to walk a certain distance into the desert by themselves and to stay there for some hours.

"The silence and solitude was new for me," he told us. "At first it was very difficult to stay there. But at last it brought me to an awareness of God's presence in a wholly new way. I know I will be different. It transformed me."

I turned to his wife Ann across the table and, half-teasing, asked, "Did it really change him, Ann?"

Dead serious, she answered, "Yes. It did."

"How can you tell?" I asked.

"Because he listens to me," she quietly answered. "I mean he really listens, not to give me a quick answer or advice but to let me know he is paying attention to what I say."

ATTENTIVENESS AND ADVENT:
LANDMARKS AND SKYLIGHTS

> No one lasts in the desert without constant attentiveness to exterior and interior landscapes alike. One must keep an eye out for landmarks. (Belden Lane)

It is Advent as I write, the time of waiting for Christ to come to us again. For one group in biblical times, Advent meant a long journey across a far desert to come to the light.

They came from a far country, these travelers. They came because they had paid attention not so much to landmarks as to a skymark—a most unusual coming together of three heavenly bodies: a star known by these ancient people as Sharu (the Babylonian word for "king") aligned with Jupiter and Venus.

This mysterious event in the eastern sky connected with their own interior landscape, a longing as ancient as light beamed from the stars, a calling to leave home in order to find their way home, to travel across an unknown landscape of barren rocks and water-less wastes, of wild desert animals and demons and barely discern-ible tracks.

These were the magi of the gospel story, the wise men from the east who Matthew tells us came to Jerusalem and asked, "Where is the one who has been born king of the Jews? We saw his star in the east and have come to worship him" (Mt 2:2 NIV). In Jerusa-lem they were directed to the prophecy of Scripture that the shep-herd of God's people would come out of Bethlehem.

So they continued on their way, and the star led them until it stopped over the place where the child was. Then, overjoyed, they bowed and worshiped him, and opened and presented to him the treasures they had brought.

Afterward they returned to their country by an alternate route. But how different the desert must have seemed on their return!

Their journey from Advent to what we now celebrate as Epiph-any has a profound symbolism for our own journey. They began their journey in the darkest time of the year, yet how piercingly clear that single star must have been in the night skies. In Bethle-hem they saw the light of eternity focused in the candlelit face of one tiny infant. Here was the light of the world, the light prophe-sied by Isaiah:

Arise, shine; for your light has come,
    and the glory of the LORD has risen upon you. . . .
Nations shall come to your light,
    and kings to the brightness of your dawn. (Is 60:1, 3)

These men came from far away to the light, so that for many cen-turies Epiphany (the twelfth day of Christmas) has been celebrated as a first glimpse of God's mission to the world, in light of the Nativity. *Epiphany* means a showing, a revelation, a making known. When we have an epiphany, it's a sudden awareness—a discovery of the crucial piece of a puzzle, a numinous experience that lights up the deepest meaning of something.

The first Epiphany story speaks powerfully to our stories. It asks: In the desert times of our world, of our heart, where do we find the landmarks or the skylights that can lead us to spiritual survival?

As a young preacher friend of mine has said, "The star is not quite enough. The star led them to Jerusalem, but only God's Word could get them to Bethlehem. A star can guide us to the target, but the Word of God gets us to the bull's-eye of Jesus Christ."

So Epiphany answers the question it raises: by telling us to pay attention to the "stars," those events of our lives that show that God has already been reaching out to us, and by paying attention to the Word of God, which takes us to where the light is brightest: the face of Jesus.

This is the most important reason of all for us to learn attentiveness. The path to attentiveness has already come to earth and is open for travel.

As my agent, Kathy Helmers, said as we discussed why it's worthwhile to learn to be attentive: "You don't have to wait until you are retired or the kids are gone to start." I would add that you don't have to wait until you get to heaven. As you learn to pay attention, it makes a difference in the here and now.

You will see things you have not seen.

You will be more fully alive.

You will experience life in its depths.

You will be more rooted, less rushing.

You will be a more whole and loving person.

You will live before you die.

Practicing Attentiveness:
What Have Been the Stars in Your Journey?

The wise men followed the star that led them to Bethlehem and to Jesus. Writer Anne Lamott describes the "lily pads"—the people, incidents, life happenings—that pointed her to God. A friend of mine speaks of the "clues" to how God is at work in our lives. Others think of them as steppingstones.

In this book I describe some of those key people, events and stages in my own life. My spiritual mentor suggested that I write down what the "images" of God have been for me as I have become more and more conscious of his presence. They range from "Jesus in my heart" as a five-year-old to the picture of a tree I climbed in college when I was feeling overwhelmed and needed a safe place. For each of them I also noted a passage from the Bible that related to them.

What have been the stars, lily pads, steppingstones, images of God in your life?

In a time of quiet, take a piece of paper and make a number of circles (or stars or lily pads or steppingstones). Try to recall any major events, happenings and persons that had a deep spiritual influence on you. Write a word or two in each circle to describe what you recall.

Some possible examples include your first prayer, sensing God in a sunset, a family crisis, a friend who influenced you, a huge disappointment, a season of doubt, something that surprised you with joy, realizing the Holy Spirit was in you.

Try to recall not just the outward event but the inner meaning it had for you—the spiritual movement that took place up or down, forward or backward.

Pause to thank God for these significant steppingstones and also to pay attention to areas in which you need more insight and growth.

One Who Paid Attention
Simone Weil on a Postage Stamp

Expectant waiting is the foundation of the spiritual life.
SIMONE WEIL

I OWE A DEBT TO SIMONE WEIL. The first time I heard of this remarkable French woman, some years ago, I read that she had defined prayer as attention. Her understanding of attentiveness was fresh and intriguing to me.

Weil died in England in 1943 at the age of thirty-three, yet left an ongoing influence in France and beyond as an apostle of the spiritual life. Many French people, including the existentialist writer Albert Camus, were deeply moved by her life and writings.

Simone Weil became a believer in Christ after a profound experience that gave birth to her understanding of attentiveness. A young Englishman had introduced her to a poem by the English metaphysical poet George Herbert, while another friend had taught her the Lord's Prayer in Greek. She learned both by heart. She was repeating to herself Herbert's poem "Love Bade Me Welcome," as she later recounted, "when the presence came." So it was out of her own life experience that she understood prayer as a special kind of attention.

Weil never became a baptized Christian; she believed that she could witness to her faith best as a kind of frontier follower of Christ, a bridge between the official church and the seeking person who was not enamored with formal religion.

It was her deep conviction that if we were once able to pray the Lord's Prayer with complete attention, we would be transformed people. She herself had the practice of saying it through once each morning "with absolute attention. If during the recitation my attention wanders or goes to sleep . . . I begin again until I have once succeeded in going through it with absolutely pure attention. . . . The effect of this practice," she testified, "is extraordinary and surprises me every time."

In her understanding, "the Our Father contains all possible petitions; we cannot conceive of any prayer not already contained in it. It is to prayer what Christ is to humanity. It is impossible to say it once through, giving the fullest possible attention to each word, without a change, infinitesimal but real, taking place in the soul."

So pervasive was Weil's influence in post–World War II France that the French government issued a postage stamp posthumously in her honor, bearing her face and inscribed with the words "Attention is the only faculty of the soul which gives us access to God."

In case our own efforts to be attentive seem to constantly fall short, Weil has a word of strong encouragement for us: "Even if our efforts of attention seem for years to be producing no result, one day a light that is in exact proportion to them will flood the soul." And knowing how difficult it is, she says, "Nothing among human things has such power to keep our gaze fixed ever more intensely upon God than friendship for the friends of God."

The Birthing Hour

Time Before Time

Whom should I turn to,
if not the one whose darkness
is darker than night, the only one
who keeps vigil with no candle,
and is not afraid.
RAINER MARIE RILKE

For darkness is as light to you.
For you created my inmost being;
you knit me together in my mother's womb.
PSALM 139:12-13 NIV

Vigils is the womb of silence, the darkest hour.
DAVID STEINDL-RAST

In the cycle of hours, Vigils, also known as Matins, is the first prayer time of each day. At Mepkin Abbey by the Cooper River in South Carolina, where I first spent several days at a monastery, Vigils takes place at 3:20 a.m. The bending live-oak trees at Mepkin remind me of monks in their white habits, stooping a bit as they walk silently through the chilly night to the chapel.

There they chant psalms, bow in prayer, listen to Holy Scripture and sit in the silence of the church, where only candles push back the shadows of the night.

As David Steindl-Rast explains in *The Music of Silence:*

The Hour of Vigils is also a symbol of the waking up we have to do in the midst of our lives. The kind of world in which we live is really a benighted world. This watching in the night and waiting for the light, this wakefulness, is a forceful reminder to wake up throughout the day from the world of sleep to another reality. . . .

Vigils, then, is the hour that calls us to set aside time outside the practical demands of the day and to connect with that dark but graced-filled mystery in which we are immersed.

My own experiences during a retreat at Mepkin Abbey, and the 3 a.m. waking, have reminded me that my day and my life begin with God who remains the same, world without end.

THE LABYRINTH

Have you ever walked a labyrinth? For many years I thought that a labyrinth was simply a kind of puzzle to solve. Then I heard that a labyrinth "prayer walk" would take place at one of our local churches. I decided to go, mostly out of curiosity.

When I arrived, on the floor of the gathering room was a very large canvas on which had been embroidered a circular design that at first glance looked like some sort of Chinese maze. Our leader for the day explained that the labyrinth was neither a game nor some New Age fad. It is a pattern embedded in the floor of an ancient cathedral in Chartres, France.

The labyrinth, she explained, is very different from a maze. Mazes are games meant to bewilder and entertain. The labyrinth, however, is a spiritual tool, a prescribed path, a sort of "embodied prayer" meant to help us put aside our chattering and cluttered mind and walk deeply in the presence of God.

She pointed to an opening on the edge of the labyrinth and suggested we begin there, then proceed at our own pace through the path, which circles back and forth and in and out, until we reached the center, which in the shape of a six-petaled rose symbolizes the six days of creation. She also suggested we reflect on our own lives during the walk, or on the life of Jesus, and that we use some word of Scripture for meditation.

I decided that I would use the time to consider my own life path, especially since I was at a point when I was seeking to shed some of the baggage and clutter of the years.

When I came to the starting place, a very odd thing happened.

I felt some kind of inner check and realized I was not ready to begin. Others stepped onto the canvas and began their walk with no hesitation, but something held me back for several minutes.

I stood puzzled, wondering what was inhibiting me. And then the thought came: Was this like my prebirth time? Was I feeling something of the apprehension that came to me as a baby, feeling the disturbing pressure that would soon thrust me out of the safety of the womb into some unknown place?

My mother was not married. The seventeen-year-old daughter of a Presbyterian minister in Canada, she had lived for nine months with what was (in those days especially, and for a clergyman's daughter) the shame of being pregnant "out of wedlock." Her mother had made all the arrangements for her to leave home until her child was born and then to return. Her father never acknowledged then or later what had happened, if he even knew.

Perhaps in those moments as I waited to start the labyrinth I was sensing some of the anxiety that she must have felt alone in Toronto, away from friends and family, her relationship ended with the man with whom she had become pregnant, her heart uncertain as to what would happen to the child she was bringing into the world.

Some words of Alan Jones help to express what I was feeling:

"The issue . . . is not so much the question of life after death as a sort of hesitation before birth. I am unwilling to allow myself to be fully alive. Parts of me are left unborn and uncared for."

If Vigils is "the womb of silence," it can recall for us the darkness of the womb in which we were formed and from which we were birthed—and remind us to pay attention to what God was doing in us long before we saw the light of day for the first time. And it can call us to pay full attention to all that God has created us to be.

The author of Psalm 139 expresses this most beautifully:

For you created my inmost being;
    you knit me together in my mother's womb.
I praise you because I am fearfully and wonderfully made;
    your works are wonderful,
    I know that full well.
My frame was not hidden from you
    when I was made in the secret place.
When I was woven together in the depths of the earth,
    your eyes saw my unformed body.
All the days ordained for me
    were written in your book
    before one of them came to be. (Ps 139:13-16 NIV)

We often speak of contemplating God. But how wonderful to think that God was contemplating us before we were born.

The psalm writer let these words lead him into his own night vigil:

How precious to [or, concerning] me are your thoughts,
        O God!
    How vast is the sum of them!
Were I to count them,
    they would outnumber the grains of sand.

When I awake,
    I am still with you. (Ps 139:17-18 NIV)

The psalm is traditionally attributed to David. Imagine him as a young shepherd boy out in the hills, away from family, lying back, looking at the night sky and perhaps saying to himself:

God is thinking of me right now, just as I am thinking of these sheep I watch over. I know their names. He knows my name! And he knew it before I was born, even before my father Jesse and my mother conceived me.

Even though I am the youngest in our family, and my brothers often ignore me and my father doesn't think I will amount to much, God doesn't ignore me.

Even if no one else ever hears of me, God knows I exist.

The Lord is my shepherd!

When I wake up in the middle of the night, sometimes I use these words from David's psalm to make that my own Vigils time and remember God's presence: "When I awake, I am still with you." The phrase reminds me to pay attention to the God who is at work in our lives even before we were born.

OUR FAMILY STORIES

As different as our personal family histories may be, they still are a good place to start paying attention.

Here is one question my family story leads me to ask: Was I "conceived in sin" as an old translation of Psalm 51:5 says? Or was it in love? I believe the latter, for I have read enough of my biological mother's journal to know how deeply she cared then for Tom, my father.

Further, I was *chosen* in love by my adoptive mother, Olive Ford, but I was twelve years old before I knew this. My mother took me for a walk in High Park in Toronto and told me, "We did not have to have you, we chose to have you." Although I was fairly old to be learning of my adoption, so far as I remember I felt neither hurt nor resentment. Instead I felt great love from her and my adoptive father, Charles.

Shortly after I was born, my mother Ford held me in her arms and presented me for dedication to Dr. Henry Frost, a veteran missionary of the China Inland Mission. "Mrs. Ford," he told her, "I believe God has given you this child for a purpose." And she, who had herself wanted to be a missionary, agreed. In a very real sense my life trajectory was set then.

Much later I would realize that her love, like all human love, had its flaws, with an obsessive side to it. Yet I think back and ask: What was God's purpose, and how should I pay attention to it?

Whatever the story of our beginnings, we can all resonate with the words of the Lord to the prophet Jeremiah:

> Before I formed you in the womb I knew you,
>> before you were born I set you apart;
>> I appointed you as a prophet to the nations. (Jer 1:5 NIV)

What God said to Jeremiah is not just for prophets and preachers! Each of us is part of a larger, longer, eternal purpose. And the dreams and desires of our parents and grandparents play a part in shaping (and, sadly, often misshaping) our beginnings.

I asked our son-in-law Craig, who is an obstetrician, how much babies are aware of in the womb.

"We know that they can hear everything that is going on around them," he told me. "For example, if a newborn baby is surrounded by a group of men, the baby will turn its head toward the father because it recognizes his voice."

He told me also of a concert pianist who while she was pregnant rehearsed a certain piece over and over in preparation for a performance. After her child was born, whenever she played that particular piece the baby would stop crying!

And, he added, while there is no scientific proof that a baby can sense the emotions its mother is feeling during the pregnancy, anxiety and stress can affect her blood pressure and the flow of blood to the placenta. So he said, "We can imagine that in the womb we can well be affected in some ways by what is going on in the emotions and mind of our mother."

The most dramatic example of a child's sensing God's presence before birth comes in the story of Mary, after she learns from an angel that she will give birth to Jesus. She hurries to share the news with the one person she can tell in confidence—her cousin Elizabeth, who is pregnant with her own son, who will be John the Baptist. When Mary enters Elizabeth's house, the baby John leaps in her womb, and Elizabeth exclaims, "Why am I so favored, that the mother of my Lord should come to me? As soon as the sound of your greeting reached my ears, the baby in my womb leaped for joy" (Lk 1:43-44 NIV).

Your own entry and mine into the world may not have been so dramatic. But as Elizabeth and the baby within her greeted Mary, God greets each of us and calls us to be special persons who live purpose-drawn lives.

The "time before our own time"—Vigils—is the time for us to address our Creator with words of thanks and openness:

Thank you, God, for creating me in my mother's womb.
Thank you for paying attention to me before I could pay
    attention to you.
Thank you for calling me, even before I was born.
Thank you for naming me even before my parents did.
And please show me: why have you chosen me?
As I reflect on my history, I ask with an open heart: for what
    purpose am I here?

VIGILS IS OVER: SLEEPY REFLECTIONS AT MEPKIN ABBEY

My alarm goes off at 3:00 a.m. I wake, close my eyes again a moment, then get up, lest I sleep in and miss the last Vigils of my retreat here at Mepkin Abbey. I dress without showering, brush my teeth and dab my wild hair with a bit of water, put on cap and windbreaker and step into the cool outside.

The moon is round and full as I walk toward the main buildings. Stars shine clearly and I whisper, "How excellent in all the earth is thy name, O Lord . . ."

A brief stop in the dining room for a half-cup of good hot coffee with honey, and then on to the white Cistercian chapel, which I left only six hours ago. Joining a handful of others, I sit in my stall, waiting. Waiting is a natural part of our rhythm of life here—waiting for prayers, for meals, for dismissal after meals. When I have found my feet hurrying to prayers, something inside me reins me in, slows me down. So we wait. A few monks in white robes and cowls filter in.

VIGIL VOICES

a distant train

an early waking bird

whistling crickets

tiny feet brushing by bushes

chants of praying men

a word of God for Joseph

(and me)

these are the voices

of Vigils.

MEPKIN ABBEY,
MARCH 19, 2002

Precisely at 3:20 a bell rings. We stand, turn, face the altar. We bow (profoundly, as we have been instructed). One of the monks invokes God's blessing.

A single note sounds on the organ. The prayer leader begins: "Praise the Lord, all you servants of the Lord, who minister by night in the house of the Lord."

Someone has prepared our psalters, marked the night readings with ribbons to guide us. The first reading is Psalm 134, our psalm each morning this week. We each have our own beautiful copy on the stand in front of us, written out in calligraphy and printed at Genesee Abbey.

After the reading we bow deeply and sing the Gloria, as we do after each psalm and hymn. Thus each closes with "World without end." I am comforted to participate in an ongoing chorus of worship flowing through ages past and years to come. I am part of something bigger, wider, deeper than my individual experience.

The community of prayer aids my weakness. When I was mind-weary yesterday, I was helped through trusting others who prayed with and alongside me, around me, for me. My solo prayers were not the whole show. Performance mattered little. Participation mattered most. I realize that we are proclaiming the Word of God across the room to each other—we are all preachers, all hearers, no "stars."

We sing antiphonally this morning, Psalms 103, 104, 105. One side chants, the other responds, two or three lines at a time. Two or three notes are all we use, carried by the murmur of the organ played unobtrusively by Abbott Klein, who was an accomplished musician. The organ notes almost echo our breathing, like the quiet motion of tides.

So we chant on: a hymn for Lent about our joyful fast. We are reminded that long faces do not attract God's grace—he wants us to lift the load, help the broken on the road. And we are reminded who made us, gave us eyes to see the full moon and stars this night. This is a long psalm about Joseph and Egypt, so long that we break it up, chant and cease. An aged brother with a long white beard takes on the role of cantor. We sing again.

Lights dim. We listen to a long reading from Exodus about plagues of flies, about gnats all over Egypt—but not in Goshen! "This is the finger of God," the panicked magicians tell Pharaoh.

Has anything changed in the Middle East?

We sit in night dimness, let the words of the story wash over us, flow in.

In the Moses-Pharaoh encounter I hear the lifelong struggle in my own soul between God's voice and all the others. The little compromises—"Go, but not too far," says Pharaoh—with which I deny reality, fudge the truth.

I think of the plagues on our lands. Traffic in drugs. Large numbers who experience depression. AIDS in Africa. Lord, when will we heed Moses?

Long silences. Waiting. No rush to fill emptiness with words. Time to think, pray. I am astounded at how clear my mind is at this hour in church!

A sermon is read—well—from Gregory Nazianzus, about God's generosity, given which how can we refuse kith and kin?

Silence again.

I thank God for the ministry of World Vision. Think it is time to give again. Wonder whether Jeanie and I are generous enough to the larger family of God in the wills we are making.

Our final prayers. We stand, say the Our Father, commend ourselves to God. We remember those who work (or suffer) in the night, we ask that Christ be their companion. We remember those who have died in the Lord.

We leave as quietly as we came. But the Great Silence is not over.

We walk silently together to our rooms, across the open spaces, under the night skies, past the bowing live oaks.

There is no word.

I touch a fellow retreatant in unspoken greeting as he goes to his room and I to mine.

The silent communion goes on.

Tomorrow what will I be doing at 3 a.m.?

Practicing Attentiveness: Sleep

When we are sleep deprived, it is difficult to pay attention: to God, others and ourselves. According to the *Harvard Health Review*, a recent survey found that more Americans are sleeping less than six hours a night, and sleep difficulties visit 75 percent of us at least a few nights per week. And it reported that sleep loss may result in irritability, impatience and the inability to be attentive.

Younger ministry leaders often come to Charlotte for a several-day retreat. When I advise them to take both long walks and lots of naps, they usually look surprised. But they are almost instantly relieved, because all of them come very tired. They are so constantly wound up that they become worn down. When we debrief at the end of the retreat, almost invariably they tell how naps and long sleeps have renewed them.

Is sleep a spiritual exercise? Yes, because we are not just spiritual beings. We are embodied spirits. Only God does not need sleep. ("He who keeps Israel will neither slumber nor sleep," said the psalmist [Ps 121:4].) But even he rested one out of seven days. God loves our bodies; he made them. And he made us to need sleep, both for our bodies and for the renewal of our souls.

The prophet Elijah, after pouring himself out in prayer to God to validate his message against the false prophets, and seeing God answer with fire, was on such a spiritual "high" that he ran twenty miles in exhilaration (1 Kings 18:46). Then when he heard that the wicked queen Jezebel was out to get him he fled to a desert place and in total exhaustion asked God to let him die. God's remedy? Sleep! He put Elijah into two long sleeps, interrupted only by rousing him to eat and drink. It was after this prolonged sleep that Elijah was led to the mountain where he could hear God's whisper (1 Kings 19).

Sleep is also a spiritual exercise because it is an expression of trust. Going to sleep is a way of admitting that we are not God, that we are very human, and that we can leave the universe (and our own small worlds) overnight in the care of the God who runs the universe. He "gives sleep to his beloved," said the psalmist (Ps 127:2). Or, as it can be translated, "He provides for his beloved during sleep."

> I will both lie down and sleep in peace;
>   for you alone, O LORD, make me like down in safety.
>   (Ps 4:8)

One Who Paid Attention
Vincent Donovan — the Masai Chief,
the Missionary and the Lion God

VINCENT DONOVAN WENT AS A MISSIONARY to the Masai people of East Africa. He went to teach them the story of God, but instead he found them teaching him.

Once he told them how God had led the nomadic Abraham to see that he was the God of all peoples and not just of one tribe. Could it be, he asked, that they had worshiped this High God without knowing him — the truly unknown God?

There was silence. Then someone asked a question. "This story of Abraham — does it speak only to the Masai? Or does it speak also to you? Has your tribe found the High God? Have you known him?"

Donovan was stumped. He thought of how in France since the time of Joan of Arc, the French people had associated God with a quest for glory. He thought of fellow Americans who had always asked God to bless "our side" in wars. After a long time he replied, "No, we have not found the High God. My tribe has not known him. For us, too, he is the unknown God. But we are searching for him. I have come a long, long distance to invite you to search for him. Let us search for him together."

Months later, as he spoke with a Masai elder about his own struggle with belief and unbelief, the elder explained that his language had two words for faith. One simply meant to agree with something. That, said the elder, was like a white hunter shooting down an animal from a distance.

To speak of real belief, he said, took another word, a word that referred to a lion going after its prey, speeding to catch it, leaping at it with a blow that kills, then enfolding it into its great arms to make it part of himself. That, said the elder, is faith.

Donovan listened in amazement. The elder continued.

We did not search you out, Padri. We did not even want you to come to us. You searched us out. You followed us away from your house into the bush . . . into our villages, our homes. You told us of the High God, how we must search for him, even leave our land and our people to find him. But we have not done this. . . . We have not searched for him. He has searched for us. He has searched *us* out and found us. All the time we think we are the lion. In the end, the lion is God.

In the end, the lion is God, the God who began to seek us even before we knew it, in the time before our time.

3  Daybreak

The Hour of Beginnings

*Oh! morning at the brown brink eastward, springs
because the Holy Ghost, over the bent
world broods with warm breast and ah! bright wings.*
GERARD MANLEY HOPKINS, "GOD'S GRANDEUR"

*Each one is a gift, no doubt,
mysteriously placed in your waking hand
or set upon your forehead
moments before you open your eyes.*
BILLY COLLINS, "DAYS"

Lauds comes just before dawn, as the first light begins to finger into the day. It is the hour that takes us from darkness into light—into the time of awakening to the day, to life, to God.

At Mepkin Abbey, Lauds begins at 5:30 a.m. As the redbirds and field creatures along the Cooper River are beginning to stir, the cowled monks and their guests make their way into the white chapel and "stand poised on the *pointe vierge* (the virginal point of the day) waiting to be called to praise." "Honor" is the significance of *laud*, but *laud* (being closely related to *lute*) also signifies a hymn of praise. This is the time when worshipers greet not only the dawn of the day but the dawn of new life, celebrating the Risen

Christ, as Christians have through many centuries, seeing in the rising sun a picture of the One who has conquered the darkness of sin and death.

Following Lauds, breakfast is served. But before Lauds the worshipers have already fed their minds and hearts with the Word of God, having spent the hour or so after Vigils in *lectio divina*, the pondering of Scripture.

"In the beginning was the Word . . ." Lauds points to the Word as the way to begin our days and the guide for our path. In the passage of life this calls to mind the early years when our identity is first being formed. In our spiritual life it is the time when we begin to wake to the light of God. It is the time of beginnings.

The first reality of day is that at dawn (and long before) God is paying attention to us. He creates each new day of our life as a gift. As day breaks, he calls us to be a people who pay attention, who watch over his world as he watches over us.

MY PERSONAL DAYBREAK

If Lauds is the time of first light, and spiritually the time of awakening to God, how does that awakening come to us?

For some the "first light" comes with the sudden startling flash of a lightning bolt. Paul is the classic example. On his way to hunt down and arrest the followers of Christ in Damascus, he was struck down by a blinding light and was himself arrested by the appearance of Jesus, who asked, "Why are you persecuting me?" Equally dramatic is the story of the young Martin Luther, weighed down by an agonized conscience, jolted to repentance when a lightning storm burst on him and almost literally knocked him off his horse. My brother-in-law Billy Graham experienced a sudden conversion during a revival meeting in his midteens, and he can cite exactly the date, time and place where it happened.

For many others the first light is less like sudden lightning and more like gradual *lightening*—the almost imperceptible coming of sunrise. This is true of Billy's late wife, Ruth, the daughter of Presbyterian missionaries to China. Ruth could not remember a time when she did not believe. Billy has mused that perhaps God led him to a wife whose experience was different from his so that he would remember that not everyone is converted suddenly at a revival meeting.

Some awaken in the drama of a Damascus Road encounter, others on the quiet journey of an Emmaus Road. These latter are like the grieving followers to whom Jesus appeared after his resurrection as they walked to Emmaus; they recognized him as he talked with them on the way and broke bread with them after they arrived.

For me it was a combination of both, but perhaps more like the sunrise.

Several years ago I went for a first meeting with my friend David, whom I was asking to be my spiritual director. The notion of a spiritual *director* may be strange to you, suggesting an expert who knows all the answers and tells us what to do. A genuine spiritual director actually does just the opposite. He or she, through discerning questions and suggestions, helps us to pay closer attention to what God is saying to us and perhaps points to things we have missed. David himself prefers to think of himself as a "spiritual friend" or companion on the journey.

At the end of that first session, David suggested a follow-up reflection: to consider what has been my image of God and how that image was formed. Indeed our image of God affects our understanding not only of God but of what we are created to be: men and women made in God's image and called to be transformed into a new image—to reflect the new "icon" of God displayed in Christ our Lord.

Almost inevitably our image of God is intertwined with the first influences on our lives, especially those of our family members, influences that come during the stage when our identity is being formed. I think of a young Korean American minister I met with at a mountain retreat. He recalled a day when he came home from school eager to tell his father what had happened there. His father briefly put down his newspaper, glanced up, made a short comment and went back to his paper. "I felt so ignored," this young man told me, "that I vowed I would never again tell my father anything that really mattered to me. And to this day I have not done so."

He began to weep. He cried in my arms for thirty to forty minutes, until my shirt was soaked and he was utterly exhausted. It was no wonder that he had had a difficult time finding a personal and caring relationship with God.

After my first session with David, my spiritual companion, I took time to think back on my family beginnings and the "first light" of my spiritual life. I wrote out three full pages of "pictures" of God, how I saw God at various stages of my life, and where these were rooted (or not!) in the stories of the Bible.

Three early mental images seemed to stand out among others: a special place in our home where my mother taught me to pray, a walk in the park where I learned I was adopted, and the figure of an absent father.

It was important for me to reflect on these images and how they were formed. For as I reflected I realized how early I had learned not to be too attentive.

LEARNING TO BE INATTENTIVE
Attentiveness is a learned practice; so is inattentiveness. I learned to be selectively inattentive, and the roots of my inattentiveness go back to my childhood.

I grew up in Chatham, Ontario, a few miles north of Lake Erie, surrounded by the farmlands of southwestern Ontario—near the places in Canada where you can look *north* to the United States! Several years ago I took our grown daughter Debbie to my old hometown. It was October, and as we drove down Victoria Avenue, the trees that gave Chatham the nickname "the Maple City" were blazing with fiery fall colors. At the corner of Gladstone and Victoria the old two-story white frame house where we lived until I was in my early teens is still standing, remodeled now into a two-family dwelling. It was in that house that my mother Ford began to shape my spiritual life and my image of God.

Olive Ford was a frustrated would-be missionary. Her childhood dream of serving God overseas was never realized, so she was committed to shaping me along those lines. The shaping involved some lengthy sessions of prayer.

At the top of the stairs in our house was an alcove where she would have me kneel on a prayer bench in front of a small lectern-like bookstand. She would hold up biographies of the missionary explorer David Livingstone or the evangelist D. L. Moody and announce earnestly, "God needs more men like this!" Then she would have me repeat after her, word for word, the prayers she wanted me to say.

So my first image of God was of a prayer bench.

During those seemingly interminable prayer sessions, I found I could escape by letting my mind wander to the outdoor hockey rink where I longed to play. I was learning to be inattentive!

My mother Ford was also a disciplinarian. She did not spank me, except once or twice. Instead she punished me with long lectures that seemed (like the prayer sessions) to last into eternity. I think I would have preferred a few swats.

"Are you listening to me, Leighton?" she would ask.

"Yes, Mother," I would assure her. "I am listening!" But during those interminable lectures I could let my mind escape into the imaginary worlds of the Chums Annual storybook I had been reading or the serial adventures of Tom Swift or Jack Armstrong I had heard on the radio. I had to learn not to pay attention. It was my only defense!

So a legacy of those childhood days was the practice of inattention.

I could focus when I wanted to. In fact, I had an innate ability to zero in for long spans on something that interested me, which made me a very disciplined student. And I did pay attention in class. That actually may have been more important for my later spiritual life than I realized. Simone Weil believed that the discipline of "school studies"—including geometry—was an important preparation for learning to pay attention to God.

I suppose my inattentiveness lay in being so preoccupied with my own thoughts that I did not learn how to give the same attention to what was going on outside of me.

Preoccupation: that term describes inattentiveness very well. A space—whether a house or a mind—that is *pre*occupied is so crowded that it has little space for anything else to enter.

Was I learning to pay attention to God? Probably. I do remember "asking Jesus into my heart" when I was five. And looking back I can see that in the hearth of my heart kindling was being laid for a fire that would later be lit.

But if I did pay attention to God back then, I would have thought he was at that prayer bench, or in the Bible passages I had to memorize, or in the confines of the Presbyterian church where, on Sunday morning when the sermon was too long, I would annoy those around me by running my fingers along the carved grooves in the pew.

I would not have expected to find God present in the unexplored depths of my young heart, in the beauty of maple leaves in the fall or the excitement of the *Hockey Night in Canada* broadcasts that I loved. Nor would I have expected him to understand the longings that I could not put into words.

One of those longings was for a present and caring father figure. My father Ford did care in his own awkward ways. But he never seemed very present; he spent most evenings away from home, bending over the watchmaker's bench at the jewelry store that he and my mother ran.

Some years ago as I worked through a course on creative writing, the longing I had sensed in early years came back to me quite powerfully. The assignment was to write something of a very personal nature that had influenced my life. I decided to write about a school costume party when I was seven or eight years old. More than anything I wanted to show up dressed as a Mountie, for I idolized the red-coated Royal Canadian Mounted Police. So I hounded my mother until somehow she found and laundered a second-hand RCMP jacket, and in it I set off proudly for the party.

But something went terribly wrong. My neck began to burn and turn red. Some of the cleaning fluid my mother had used was still permeating the collar, and it was scalding my neck. Before long it hurt so badly that I had to leave. I fled in tears, running home as fast as I could.

My first draft of that story was factual but not compelling. A writing friend suggested I do a rewrite, telling the story to myself as if I were my own audience.

Shortly after I was waiting for our son Kevin at arrive at the Toronto airport for a visit to my childhood home. As I waited outside the airport, I decided to tell the story to myself. As I did, I remembered so vividly the disappointment of that little boy that I felt tears coming. Oblivious to any passersby, I reached around with my arms and literally hugged myself, imagining I was my own father.

It's all right, I told myself. *It's going to be all right. Let's go fishing.*

I never remember my father hugging me like that. And we never did go fishing.

As an adopted boy I did realize that I had been chosen and was loved. But still there was a yearning—what Frederick Buechner describes as "a longing for a long time from a long way off to belong." As I grew up with a mother who was all too present (and later almost disappearing) and a father who was emotionally absent, that yearning was very deep.

In those formative years, I was an introvert, a boy who entertained myself through the inner life of mind and imagination, who found an escape route from Mother's lectures and learned to be attentive mainly to his own preoccupations.

I remember my childhood as a happy one. But I did have a lot to learn—and unlearn.

BEGINNING TO PAY ATTENTION

Shortly after I turned fourteen, in the winter of 1945, my mother left home. Where she had gone and why was a mystery to me. Many years later, I learned from one of my professors that she suffered from the mental disorder we call paranoia and that she lived with many fears.

My mother was gone for months. She chose to go to Winnipeg, Manitoba, where she lived in disguise and under an assumed name. That June, World War II ended, and that summer I came to attention as never before.

Mother had returned in late spring. She became interested in a new Bible conference that a local businessman was starting a few miles away on the St. Clair River. We began attending sessions there, and some nights I stayed over in one of the simple cabins on the grounds.

Two things impressed me. One was the lively faith of a group of young people on the staff. Something about the way they sang and prayed together drew me—and there was also one very cute girl named Betty whom I liked but was too shy to talk to. I was also riveted by the messages of the speaker, a fiery preacher from Toronto who looked, I imagined, like an Old Testament prophet with his striking combed-back white hair, his startling Viking-like blue eyes, and a thin finger that would jab his points home.

What brought me to full attention was the night he told us how he prayed.

"I am full of nervous energy," he said. "I can't sit or stand still long. If I kneel I get restless. So when I pray I walk up and down."

A light flashed on: I didn't have to kneel at that prayer bench! I could pray and get exercise at the same time.

"When I pray silently my mind wanders," he went on. "So I say my prayers out loud."

He was speaking my language, and he had more to offer. "I was saying the same old words over and over and got tired of it. So now I take my Bible, turn to a passage, perhaps one of the psalms, and turn the words into my prayer."

His words lit a fire of imagination deep within me. I knew I wanted to know God as more than a name, in a living and personal way.

Early the next morning I made my way to a woods on the edge of the grounds and began to walk up and down and pray out loud. I am sure I was self-conscious. What would anyone who saw me have thought? But I was not deterred. I let my Bible fall open to Psalms and flipped through until I found one that seemed right for me. It may have been one of David's cries for help, like Psalm 42:

My soul thirsts for God,
   for the living God
When shall I come and behold
   the face of God?

I turned words like those into my own, words of a lonely, confused fourteen-year-old, words perhaps like these:

God, I am thirsty for you.
I need you like a drink of water on one of these hot
   summer days.
You know how confused I have been, wanting something.
I don't know what's going on with Mom and Dad.
I think what I want is you . . . but how do I find you?
When will I ever come and know you as these other kids do?

There was no sudden voice or light. But there was some sense of
quiet confirmation that the prayer spoken in heartfelt honesty had
been heard.

Somehow, from somewhere, a *yes* was spoken in my heart.

It was an awakening moment. And it was more. I was looking
more closely, more deeply, than I ever had at the green of the trees
and the blue of the river, at the Word in the words of the Bible, the
word in nature, the Word coming into my heart. It was truly—
though I did not know this term at the time—an experience that
brought an awareness of God's presence in all things.

Many years later when I read the French philosopher Emile
Caillet's account of his own discovery of the Bible as "the book that
understood me," I thought, *That was my experience too.* I might
also have described what I found in the words of a hymn my
mother had taught me:

Heaven above is softer blue,
Earth beneath is sweeter green;

Something glows in every hue
Christless eyes have never seen.

Birds with sweeter songs o'erflow,
Flowers with deeper beauties shine,
Since I know, as now I know,
I am his, and he is mine.

Recalling those words now, I find them overly sentimental, and
they are by no means great hymnody. But they did express then
what was a genuine awakening in my own soul, "seeing God in all
things, and all things in God."

It was the beginning of a journey of coming to attention, a seed
sown that would bear fruit much later in my life.

AWAKENINGS

How then do we begin to come to attention to a God who is there?
Is there a formula, a set of instructions? None I am sure that
"work" just right for everyone. I suppose it is more like waking
from sleep or, even more, awakening to love and beauty.

What is it like when I wake up in the morning? I am not aware
that my subconscious is saying, *Wake up, wake up.* Unless an
alarm is ringing, there is usually just the realization: *Sleep is over,
I am awake.* It just comes, and my eyes open to the new day. Falling is love is very much the same. We don't plan, *Today I will fall
in love.* We see, we meet, we talk, we listen, and scientists tell us
the "mirror neurons" in our brains actually align with those of another person—in this case someone we are beginning to love, and
hopefully theirs align with ours. It's both biology and poetry.

So we begin a day with a yawn and a stretch. And we begin a
love with a few stammering words. In both instances the question
comes: what do we see?

Someone suggested to me that as God knows what we really

love, he uses these loves to waken us.

A friend, who was a student both of archaeology and of art history, was in grad school and found her first glimmer of longing for God's light in a museum in Munich, when she saw a painting of a blue horse by Franz Marc. It was only a momentary glimpse. Years later, as her spiritual search truly began, the memory of that painting took her back to a long-forgotten childhood story of a girl led home by a horse. Later, in a chapel in Taos, New Mexico, she was reawakened by a painting of Christ whose eyes followed her wherever she moved. Across the years God used these glimpses to draw her to a greater love.

Francis Collins, the eminent scientist who heads the Human Genome Project, relates his own awakening in terms of both moral reason and revelation. Brought up in a highly ethical but nonreligious family, he gave little thought to God until he was in his medical residency. An older patient told him she could not have borne her illness without her faith and asked, "What do you believe in, doctor?" He realized he had no answer, had given the question little thought. Eventually the writings of C. S. Lewis convinced him that the universe has a moral imperative beyond himself, and his scientific explorations brought him to see DNA as part of "the language of God."

The sense that God was reaching out to him came in an almost mystical experience while he was mountain climbing in the northwestern United States. On a hillside he saw three streams rushing down the rocks and forming one great waterfall below. To him it seemed a symbol of the Trinity—three in one! That brought this man of science to his knees and his faith.

This, I believe, is the path of awakening: the God who loved us before we were born, in whom we live and move and have our being, reaches out to us in the ways he knows will best awaken the seed that has been planted in us from eternity. As Paul told the philosophers on Mars Hill, God allots our times and places so that we will "search for God and perhaps grope for him and find him—though indeed he is not far from each one of us" (Acts 17:27).

The first step on the path to awakening may be simply to pray: "Lord, open my eyes, that I may see."

Practicing Attentiveness: First Thoughts

C. S. Lewis said that when he first woke, thoughts came rushing in like a thousand wild animals all clamoring for attention. I understand that!

So I have tried (and am still trying) to let my first thoughts—or at least some of my first thoughts—be toward God. For example, on awaking I often pray parts of Psalm 25:

> To you, O LORD, I lift up my soul;
> in you I trust, O my God. . . .
> Show me your ways, O LORD,
> teach me your paths;
> guide me in your truth and teach me,
> for you are God my Savior,
> and my hope is in you all day long. (vv. 1-2, 4-5 NIV)

For a while I had those words taped to the mirror in my bathroom to read as I shaved. (I also had them taped to the windshield of my car for a time, until a worried passenger asked if that was because I tended to have accidents!)

Or I may use words of Dietrich Bonhoeffer:

> O God, early in the morning I cry to you.
> Help me to pray
> and to concentrate my thoughts on you;
> I cannot do this alone.

Often in the morning I will sit in a favorite chair in my study with a cup of coffee, with classical music playing, not trying to form a prayer with words but waiting, listening, until perhaps I sense the Spirit bringing to the surface a word from God. Then I offer just a simple "Thank you." I have found this time of silence, even if it is very short, to be a key to starting the day with attention.

Many days I walk early with my Australian cattle dog, Wrangler, in woods near our house or on a schoolyard track next door. Often this is a time to pray over and over a version of the Jesus Prayer, "Lord Jesus Christ, Son of God, have mercy on me—and on your world."

As I walked early one day near Grandfather Mountain, North Carolina, the sun, like the psalmist's bridegroom (Ps 19:5), came leaping through the clouds to backlight the hills, and a prayer of John Wesley came to my lips:

> Thou brightness of th' eternal glory,
> unto thee is my heart,
> though without a word,
> for my silence speaketh unto Thee.

PRAYER IS LIKE WATCHING FOR THE KINGFISHER

Prayer is like watching for
The kingfisher. All you can do is
Be there where he is like to appear, and
Wait.
Often nothing much happens;
There is space, silence and
Expectancy.
No visible signs, only the
Knowledge that he's been there
And may come again.
Seeing or not seeing cease to matter,
You have been prepared.
But when you've almost stopped
Expecting it, a flash of brightness
Gives encouragement.

ANN LEWIN

That has often been my prayer on bright mornings! It has helped me to start the day by using familiar words. But just as often my prayer may be a simple greeting: "God, I am here!"

The exact form does not matter. What matters is the reality. In the words of C. S. Lewis: "The prayer preceding all prayers is this, May it be the real I who speaks. May it be the real Thou that I speak to."

If you're like me, there are times of prayer when nothing much seems to happen. Perhaps Ann Lewin's poem "Prayer Is like Watching for the Kingfisher" will speak to you as it does to me. Don't forget to wait!

One Who Paid Attention
The Teacher Who Took Off His Hat

IN SEMINARY MY BIBLE PROFESSOR was Manfred George Gutzke, a Canadian like myself, who had an impressively large physique and had been the boxing champion of the Canadian Army in his youth. Everything about him seemed oversized: his huge hairless head, his enormous eyebrows, his low gravelly voice, his sweeping knowledge of the Scriptures.

Not only did he hold us spellbound with his grasp of the Bible; he also fascinated us with stories out of his own life, which he often told over a game of crokinole when he and his wife invited us students to spend an evening in their home.

Manfred Gutzke was a man of God, as well as a teacher of preachers, but he had not started out religious in any formal sense. For many years he was an agnostic. Yet in the years when he was teaching in a one-room rural school on the prairies of western Canada, he began to be a seeker, wondering whether there might be a God and he could know him.

He was especially impressed by a devout farmer who moved into that small community. This man sold two cows and donated the proceeds to missionary work on the annual missions Sunday. This was cause for amazement at the small prairie church, where most of the farmers came because there was nothing better to do on a Sunday morning. Most of them stood outside and gossiped with their friends until long after the service began. But this new man arrived carrying a Bible, went straight into the church and bowed his head in prayer.

Here was someone whose faith seemed central, and the young teacher was intrigued.

One afternoon after school, making his way across the fields to his boarding house, he was struck by this thought: *If God exists, then he can see me right now!*

"I stood in that field," he told us, "and pondered that thought. If God exists, he could see me.

"So," he said, "I took off my hat! That may seem strange, but like most men in those days I wore a brimmed hat, and I always took it off in the presence of women, older people or other important persons. So I took my hat off to God.

"And then I prayed: 'God, I do not know whether you are there or not. And I don't mean anything bad by that. I just don't know. But I want to know, and you know that too. So please show me if you are real.'

"I felt," he said, "as if something very important had happened."

Then he put his hat back on and made his way home.

He had taken a first step toward his spiritual home that day. For the very first time Manfred Gutzke paid attention to God—the God who was already paying attention to him. And before much more time had passed, he would come to prove in his own life the affirmation of Jesus, "Seek and you shall find," and the promise in Hebrews 11:6 of a God who "rewards those who earnestly seek him" (NIV).

4   Prime Time
Our Root System

*Prime is that hour of the day when we pray
not to get it over with, but to make everything a prayer.*
DAVID STEINDL-RAST

We pray the work.
MOTHER TERESA

O ne of my fond memories of Mepkin Abbey is of a monk on a rickety old bicycle, his robe flapping around him, pedaling off toward his morning duties in the vegetable garden. Others were headed for their tasks in the kitchen, the library or the gift store. It was off to work for them after observing Prime, the hour of deliberate beginning of the day.

Prime has been called "the drum roll of the day," a reminder to work not just to get it over with but for its own sake. Too often we rush into things and hurry through them, and Prime resists this tendency. It reminds us that, whatever we do, we should begin it thoughtfully and do it with a whole-hearted attention. As David Steindl-Rast puts it, "During Prime, we commit ourselves to do everything today in the same way that we teach children to cross a street: stop, look, then go."

The Prime time of our lives moves perhaps from the earlier years of education and preparation into the time when we begin to discover and settle into our work, the way we make a living and, more important, make a life.

Spiritually, Prime might be the time when, like young Samuel in the Bible, we hear God's voice in his Word and Spirit and answer, "Speak, Lord, your servant hears." It is the time when we respond to "the voice of this calling" and seek to discern and follow our mission.

Before we launch into life or rush into the day, do we take time to be sure our "root system" is in place, that we are "rooted and grounded" in love (Eph 3:14-17)?

The lovely North Carolina mountain town of Blowing Rock (the mythical Mitford of Jan Karon's novels) is the setting of one of my favorite walks. A block from the busy main street, a quiet path by a stream begins level, then descends steeply through Glen Burney to the cascade and the falls below. The trail is shaded by huge old trees and bounded at many points by large rocks.

One day a friend and I were making our way slowly back up from the falls when we noticed two hardwood trees standing on top of a huge boulder. We were amazed that they could grow there, let alone endure through the snow and winds of winter.

"How do they manage to live?" I asked. Then we noticed that while the trunks of the two trees clearly rose from the top of the boulder, their twin root systems snaked down and around the rock, finding their way into the ground through a cleft to gain firm support.

The day before I had been struggling with my thoughts on the significance of Prime and had been frustrated as I tried to find a metaphor for this hour of beginning. Now these trees on a rock became a parable of nature. As we looked at this ingenious root system, it seemed to pose a question: *What is the root system of my life? Is it deep and wide and long and strong enough to withstand the pressures of each day?* That is the paramount question at the hour of Prime.

Jesus' picture of himself as the vine and of us as branches came to me, reminding me that we can be fruitful and productive only as we remain connected to the vine. "Abide in me," he said to his disciples (see Jn 15). "Remain in me, stay at home with me" is the centering thought.

The intertwining of Celtic knots also came to mind: wreaths of leaves intricately woven together.

Abiding is one of three words that aptly sum up the intent of Prime, along with *indwelling* and *contemplation.* Let's explore the three, for they are closely connected.

WHAT DOES IT MEAN TO BE CONTEMPLATIVE?

For many of us when we hear the word *contemplative,* we think of a monk, sitting for hours, eyes closed, hands folded, lost to the world around. Of course such a monk is indeed a contemplative. But the idea of being contemplative is much bigger.

Contemplate is a two-part word, compounded from the Latin *con* (meaning "with") and *templum* (temple), thus to observe things within a special place, and especially to observe in the presence of a deity. So a contemplative is one who *looks at life in the presence of God,* or we might say with the eyes of God, or through the eyes of Christ—at any time, not just at special times; anywhere, not just in certain places; toward anyone, not just "special" people.

Consider how a poet, a spiritual teacher and a psychiatrist think of contemplation.

The poet Kathleen Norris believes "the true mystics of the quotidian are not those who contemplate holiness in isolation, reaching godlike illumination in serene silence, but those who manage to find God in a world filled with noise, the demands of other people and making a living."

Pastor and teacher Eugene Peterson understands contemplation simply as living by the biblical revelation. "It has nothing to do with whether we spend our days as a grease monkey under an automobile or on our knees in a Benedictine choir. . . . The contemplative life is not a special kind of life; it is the Christian life, nothing more but also nothing less. But *lived*."

For psychiatrist David Benner, contemplation is "wordless openness to the world," knowing the heart of things by "the way of wonder . . . a way of knowing that is intuitive with children."

I am sure I saw one of Benner's child contemplatives one summer in Vancouver as I sat on a bench at the seawall on the edge of English Bay. Along came a mother and infant son. He—dressed in a navy-blue sweatshirt and a gray-brimmed hat—caught my attention when he suddenly whispered, "Oh, oh."

He had spotted a drainage grate set into the paved walkway and was fascinated. I watched, entranced, as he peered into it, then picked blades of grass and dropped them one at a time through the bars of the grate. His mother waited, patiently, wise enough to indulge his curiosity.

I could almost see his little mind thinking, *Oh. Down. Where does it go?*

Soon his father caught up and, seeing me watching, explained, "We just got off a flight from Europe, and our time is skewed." For his son, it was clear that, whatever the time change, there was no rush.

"He doesn't need a TV to keep him happy," I said.

"We don't have one," said Father.

Ha! I thought. *An imagination sprouts!*

The great irony of our wired age of communication is that many of our children are growing up information rich and imagination poor—and so are many adults. As I watched that boy with his wordless wonder, I asked myself: *Do I ever stop, with a mind like a child, to look at the unexpected openings in my path, drop my blades of grass and wonder where they go? Or have I lost that sense of imagining wonder?* Much of the time I have to confess I am only half looking, and half seeing, too preoccupied with my thoughts, running from what has been to what will be next, really to live in the present.

Slowly, so slowly, I am learning, even at this stage of my life, to observe my own version of Prime before I start the day's work. It may be just a short walk with my dog Wrangler by a nearby stream, standing still, looking at the sky and trees, breathing in the fresh air, remembering to stop, and look, before I go.

And often I pause to lift this prayer of St. Fursey:

The arms of God be around my shoulders,
The touch of the Holy Spirit upon my head,
The sign of Christ's cross upon my forehead,
The sound of the Holy Spirit in my ears,
The fragrance of the Holy Spirit in my nostrils,
The vision of heaven's company in my eyes,
The conversation of heaven's company on my lips,
The work of God's church in my hands,
The service of God and the neighbor in my feet,
A home for God in my heart,
And to God, the father of all, my entire being.
Amen.

WHAT DOES IT MEAN TO ABIDE?

If to contemplate means to look at life in the presence of God, to see with fresh-washed eyes, then how do I stay in touch during this day, and all the days of my life?

Princeton scholar Robert Wuthnow has suggested that the current interest in "spirituality" takes two forms. One is a kind of free-floating, rootless fascination with all things "spiritual." The other he characterizes as "abode-oriented"—finding a home in centuries-old practices and grounded in the realities of daily life.

Abode immediately suggests *abiding*, and abiding is vital to Christian spirituality. Our imagination may dance like the waving branches of a tree, but our reality must be as grounded as the trees I saw growing on and around the rock near the Carolina mountain stream. Here again is Jesus' own picture: "I am the true vine. . . . Abide in me as I abide in you. Just as the branch cannot bear fruit by itself unless it abides in the vine, neither can you unless you abide in me. I am the vine, you are the branches" (Jn 15:1, 4-5).

I must have read and thought about these words hundreds of time across the years. Beginning in my teens I wondered what *abiding* meant. It seemed to convey the very cozy sense that a grandfatherly person would have sitting at home, perhaps by the fire on a winter afternoon, Bible on his lap, cat or dog at his feet, enjoying a cup of tea and feeling very peaceful, letting nothing disturb these quiet moments, thinking very pleasant spiritual thoughts.

But what did coziness have to do with the active mind and life of a teenager, or later for an anxious father or hurried minister, or his stay-at-home wife with sick children? Or with a world torn apart by war, worn down by poverty?

Abiding, like contemplation, must have a more robust sense. And it does.

Imagine that you are one of Jesus' disciples, chosen to be with him in that very private upper room gathering just before his crucifixion. You are taken aback when he picks up a towel and basin and goes around the circle washing your feet, and then tells you to serve the others as he has served you, to love one another as he has loved you. He startles you even more when he announces, "One of you will betray me." You glance around at the others, deeply disturbed. Then he tells you that he is going where you can't come.

"Why not?" bursts out Peter. "I would lay down my life for you. Why can't I go with you?" In your heart you are asking the same question.

"Don't be troubled," responds Jesus gently, reassuringly. "In my Father's house are many dwelling places. . . . I am going to prepare one for you. . . . I will come again and take you to myself, so that where I am, there you will be also."

A "dwelling place"—but what kind of abode is that to be? Shortly you hear him use the same word again, this time as a verb. "Rise," he says, "let us be on our way," and then he adds, "Abide in me." How, you wonder, can you do both—stay and go?

Then you begin to catch just a glimpse of what Jesus is saying. He has promised a coming home with the Father down the road. But now he promises a home *on* the road! "Let us rise and go . . . but let us abide." Going and abiding belong together. Once his mission is complete—and you still do not understand all about what is ahead for him, the cross, the resurrection and the ascending to his Father—then you too will be on mission. And on that mission his presence will be with you. "Be at home in me," he is saying, "as I make my home with you. Stay with me, as I stay with you."

A few days later, when you gather again in that upper room with your friends, grieving the death of your Lord, you look up and there he is: Jesus, present and very real. "Peace," he says, and when he holds out his hands you can see the wounds made by the nails. Once more he reminds you of your mission and his promise. "As my Father has sent me, so I send you." Then he breathes on you and says, "Receive the Holy Spirit" (Jn 20:22).

His words are the promise that he will "indwell" you just as God had been present with your ancestors through the long centuries.

The late Lesslie Newbigin captured this meaning of *abiding* beautifully:

The gracious indwelling of God with his people is not an invitation to settle down and forget the rest of the world: it is a summons to mission, for the Lord who dwells with his people is the one who goes before them in the pillar of fire and the cloud. So the promise of his presence is clinched in the words, "Up, let us go hence." There is a mission to be fulfilled. There is a conflict to be waged with the powers of this world. There is tribulation to be endured.

Now you begin to understand the true sense of "abiding." It is not an invitation to a cozy time by the fire (although those times will also be welcome). It is a summons to stick with him on the way, wherever that may lead, and the promise that whatever comes he will stay with you.

The Anabaptist scholar David Rensberger, reflecting on the persecution faced by his spiritual ancestors, sees abiding as having both an inward and an outward dimension:

> Inwardly, it is a ceaseless orientation toward Jesus, a constant looking to him, listening for his voice, seeking his ways. Outwardly, it appears as an enduring persistence in this orientation, refusing every temptation to turn elsewhere for security, companionship, or hope. . . . To abide in Jesus is to place Jesus, both devotion to him and discipleship to him, above all else. It means letting other voices, other invitations—to profit, to pleasure, sometimes even to safety and self-preservation—go unheeded. It means a humble, gentle persistency in attending to Jesus and only to him, and a kind of unyielding yieldedness to him alone.

WHAT IS MEANT BY *INDWELLING*?

One who has spoken compellingly about "indwelling" as the way we know almost everything is the late Hungarian scientist/philosopher Michael Polanyi. Already a world-class physicist, in the 1930s Polanyi turned his attention to the philosophy of science.

In his influential book *The Tacit Dimension* he told of a conversation he had with a leading Soviet scientist who said that the Union of Soviet Socialist Republics saw science as useful only to advance socialism by rationally conceived five-year plans. Polanyi was dismayed at the limits of this version of how scientists work and how it overlooked the powerful role of intuition.

Polanyi envisioned science as an "indwelling" of what the scientist tacitly knows and discovers, as opposed to a purely rational objectivity. "We always know more than we can tell" was one key idea at the heart of his philosophy. The other was "indwelling." We know because we "indwell" the thing we know, and in a sense it indwells us.

Indwelling, observed Polanyi, takes place in the way we know other people—getting inside their skin by an act of empathy. It happens in the way we take in a work of art. As we look at its surface, we somehow enter into the mind of its creator. Indwelling happens when we internalize moral values, not merely assenting unquestioningly to the teachings of our parents or society.

Indwelling brings home to us "that it is not by looking at these things, but by dwelling in them, that we understand their meaning." Parents know their children in this way. And lovers their beloved. The skillful technician, athlete or musician also enters into his work via indwelling.

I once asked my son-in-law, Craig, a fine obstetrician/gynecologist, how he makes diagnoses. "You've got years and years of training and experience, a huge cache of knowledge and tools," I said. "How much of that is in the forefront when a patient comes to you complaining of a problem?"

"Not much," he said. "I don't use checklists much unless it's a really difficult problem. What I want to do is to really listen to my patient, try to sense what may be out of balance in her whole body. Then I instinctively draw on all the knowledge and experience."

When I told him that I was gnawing on Polanyi's idea of indwelling, he exclaimed, "Tacit knowing! I read that in college. It put so much together for me, helped me to see the work and the human body as much more than the sum of its parts." Craig is indwelling both his technical knowledge and his patients. He has allowed his skills to become like the stick in the blind man's hand, a part of himself with which he reaches out to touch the reality of his patient, to see and hear and know her, so to speak, to indwell her body and soul and even her disease.

Polanyi's thought is important, and not only as a philosophical point. It has implications for the attention we as Christ-followers pay in the "secular" parts of our everyday lives, not only in our devotional times.

The Scottish theologian Thomas Torrance, a close friend of Polanyi and a key interpreter of his work, sees a vital connection between Polanyi's concept of indwelling and Jesus' teaching about abiding. All of our work is best accomplished through a process of "tuning in" or indwelling. Torrance, who often spoke with Polanyi about matters of faith, is convinced that Polanyi's concept of indwelling finds its source in Scripture.

"This strange notion of indwelling," he says, "comes from John's Gospel—the notion of dwelling and abiding in Christ."

So indwelling joins abiding and contemplation as means of attentiveness in the Prime time of our lives.

Abiding and *indwelling* are almost synonyms. Some translators render Jesus' words in John 15:4 as "Abide in me as I abide in you," others as "Dwell in me as I dwell in you." Still others translate them as "Remain in me as I remain in you." Whatever the translation, the vital reality is that Jesus and his disciples share a common life, as do a vine and its branches.

The thought of God's "indwelling" his people runs like a golden thread through the Bible, from David's prayer of longing to dwell in God's tent (Ps 61:4), through the prophet Isaiah's promise that God the "high and lofty one" will "dwell . . . with those who are contrite and humble in spirit" (Is 57:15), to the birth of Emmanuel ("God with us," Mt 1:23 NIV), on to the apostle's proclamation of the mystery of "Christ in you, the hope of glory" (Col 1:27), and finally to the vision of John the seer of the time when "the home of God is among mortals. He will dwell with them" (Rev 21:3).

But what is the link between the God who is our eternal dwelling place, to whom hungry spirits long to go, and the God whose transforming presence finally dwells in every nook and cranny of all creation? John's gospel story gives us the key: the arrival of the One whose dwelling was with God, who has come to pitch his tent among us and now dwells through his Spirit in those who by faith enter a living relation of loving obedience to him. In John's story "indwelling" becomes a matrix in which all relationships meet.

The same intimacy that the Father and Son share will be available to Jesus' followers, for, he tells them, "[the Spirit] abides with you, and he will be in you" (Jn 14:17). He promises that "those who love me will keep my word, and my Father will love them, and we will come to them and make our home with them" (Jn 14:23).

Indwelling is an imperative for living this new and abundant life. "Abide in me and I in you," Jesus commands, picturing branches drawing life from their "dwelling" in their vine's trunk. So abiding is both an established and an ongoing relationship. Abiding, writes Newbigin, "is the continually renewed decision that what has been done once for all by the action of Jesus shall be the basis, the starting point, the context for all my thinking and deciding and doing."

How do we make this continually renewed decision? By letting Jesus' words dwell deeply in us. "If you abide in me, and my words abide in you, ask for whatever you wish, and it will be done for you," said Jesus. And what follows from this abiding? Our prayers will be answered, the Father will be glorified, and we will bear abundant fruit and be recognized as Jesus' disciples (Jn 15:7-8).

And how is that fruit recognized?

It will simply be the life of Jesus being made visible in the midst of the life of the world.

A LIFE OF CONTINUAL CONVERSATION

When I consider these three important words, I confess I feel just a bit bewildered. If contemplation (seeing life in the presence of God), abiding in Christ, and Christ's indwelling me are so important, how do they operate in my everyday life?

How do I take these wonderful concepts and translate them into my own "prime time"?

How can I actually dwell in Jesus and his words—and have them dwell in me?

It helps me to think of "abiding" as a continual conversation in which I listen for God's voice and speak back to him. The late Henri Nouwen said that to "pray without ceasing" would be impossible if it meant that we did nothing but think and speak constantly about God. To pray unceasingly is not to think about God rather than other things, or to talk to God instead of to other people, but rather to think, speak and live in the presence of God. Prayer, Nouwen continued,

> can only become unceasing prayer when all our thoughts— beautiful or ugly, high or low, proud or shameful, sorrowful or joyful—can be thought and expressed in the presence of God. . . . This requires that we turn all our thoughts into con-

versation. The main question, therefore, is not so much what we think, but to whom we present our thoughts. . . . Prayer is an outward, careful attentiveness to the One who invites us to unceasing conversation.

Through this kind of conversation life becomes a kind of ongoing *lectio divina,* a rhythm of listening for God's voice in Scripture (and also through his Spirit in nature, and our own hearts) and answering back in whatever kind of response is appropriate—in word, action or even ongoing silence.

Prime should be the time of listening first not to my needs and wants but to Jesus' words and directions. Prime can be early in life, early in our life with Christ and early in the day. I am blessed that when I was very young and impatient my adopted mother Ford taught me to memorize parts of the Bible, words that still come back to me again and again. I am also blessed that in my early teens I learned to "pray the Scriptures" as a way to be formed as a disciple of Jesus. And I am blessed every morning when I can quietly sit in the presence of my Lord, waiting for his voice, hearing from his Word and then moving into the day knowing that as I go with him I also stay with him: abiding in him and in his Word.

This way of living—of listening and responding to the words of Jesus—is not just a matter of learning what Jesus said, or even asking the well-known question WWJD: what would Jesus do? It is a way of opening myself to ask WIJD: what is Jesus doing? The apostle Paul certainly knew what Jesus said, but he quoted Jesus directly only three times. It was the word of Jesus living in him that changed him.

To paraphrase another writer, I know the transforming power of Christ not only because once he said to his disciples in an upper room, "Love one another as I have loved you" but because now he is loving through me by his Spirit living in me.

LOVE AS FOCUSED ATTENTION

What difference can Prime make as we begin and go through our days? When Jesus spoke of abiding, it was all about loving obedience, being loved by him and loving others as he loved us. We might describe love—whether the love is that of friendship or of lovers or of compassion—as *focused attention*.

In friendship, out of a potential universe of candidates, we select (or have selected for us, as Augustine said, in a kind of "divine lottery") certain ones on whom we focus time and attention. In the practice of attentiveness we are able to see and be blessed by the beauty of the friend.

In married love we pledge to each other that singular attention signified in the biblical word *cleaving*—"therefore a man leaves his father and his mother and cleaves to his wife, and they become one flesh" (see Gen 2:24 RSV). *Cleave* here is used in the old English sense of the word, meaning a bonding together. It is more than the attention of moonstruck lovers gazing into each other's eyes. It is the faithful attention of two lives committed to each other in sickness and in health, in joy and in sorrow, in abundance and in scarcity, in times of light and times of darkness.

It is this undivided attention to each other that sustains and strengthens us in our vocation of love to family and neighbors and friends.

In all these relationships the attention paid is not possessive. It is an attention that is freeing, not paralyzing. That is the kind of compassionate love with which Christ companions us as we meet others in need.

Focused love is powerfully portrayed in Ben Long's fresco *The Good Samaritan* at First Presbyterian Church in Charlotte, North Carolina. Some time ago I sat gazing at it with a friend and asked, "Where is the center of the painting? Is it in the robbers off to one

side, dividing their loot? Or in the distant figures of the priest and
Levite, passing by the wounded traveler and walking on engrossed
in their own conversation?" Clearly not. Our eyes were drawn
front and just off center to the face of the ravaged traveler, his eyes
looking up toward the kindly face of the Samaritan, who gazes
down at him with deep compassion.

The dazed look of the one seems to say, "Who are you? What are
you doing?"

And the caring look of the other seems to respond, "I am here
for you."

That much was clear as we contemplated the fresco. But my
friend was paying even closer attention and after a moment of silence said, "I think the center is in the empty space between the
face of the Samaritan and the face of the traveler."

That was exactly right. There was a power in the short distance
that separated their faces, just at the moment when their eyes were
meeting, an invisible force that made me think of the poet Rainer
Maria Rilke's description of "the love that consists in this: that two
solitudes protect and border and salute each other."

The painting spoke to me about the mutuality and the boundaries of attentive love.

Too close, and our individuation is blurred.

Too distant, and the dynamic tension inherent in love is lost.

But through the mediation (and really the Mediator) of focused
love, connection happens.

Prime, then, is a focal point as we begin our work. We are reminded of the focused and attentive love of God who sent his Son
into the world, loving not from a distance but from up close, yet
loving us in such a way that our personhood is not obliterated but
renewed. Through the lens of Christ we are able to look into the
face of God and to be changed into his image, "from one degree of

glory to another" (2 Cor 3:18). And through that same lens we begin to look into the faces of those we meet, and we see them too as potential carriers of the image and glory of Christ.

Marvin, a lawyer friend in Wichita, Kansas, adopted this practice. Marvin came to faith when he was well along in his professional life as a litigator. "I used to look at opposing counsel and their clients as opponents, targets," he says. "But after Christ came into my life, the people across the table had faces."

Marvin had come to know the essence of Prime time.

Practicing Attentiveness: Lectio Divina

Lectio divina is an ancient practice of listening to God and responding. Although it dates back perhaps to the twelfth century, there are many followers of Christ in the twenty-first century who have not been exposed to it. Although I unwittingly practiced a kind of "lectio" when I was only fourteen, I was introduced to it more fully only a dozen or so years ago. *Lectio divina* —literally, "divine reading" —consists of four movements: *lectio* (reading a passage out loud several times and asking "What does it say?"); *meditatio* (reflecting on the text, and perhaps just on a phrase or two, to ask "What does it say to me?"); *oratio* (praying back to God, whether out loud or silently, my response); and *contemplatio* (resting in the presence of the One who stands in and behind the text).

Lectio is a very good practice for daily Prime, for a word heard from God as we begin the day may call us back to "abide, stay, be at home" many times as the day continues to unfold. Those very words, *abide, stay, be at home,* have been key words for me now for several months.

One Who Paid Attention
My Spiritual Director Dog

I HAVE THOUGHT OF MY AUSTRALIAN Cattle Dog Wrangler as many things—a Blue Heeler, a curious and always hungry dog, a great buddy. But never as a spiritual director. That is, until a recent Sunday.

It had been a very cold night, so I had let Wrangler sleep inside. When I woke and was saying a morning prayer, he got as close to me as he could, then went out to eat.

I continued a time of reflection, reading an article by David Benner on the practice of contemplative prayer, which he describes as the dance of "being with God": "Prayer in all its forms is nothing more than a response to the Divine invitation to friendship. Contemplative prayer is simply offering ourselves in faith and openness to God, spending time in silence with our Beloved, who, we dare to trust, longs to spend that time with us."

The previous month had been very, very full, and I had felt in a kind of spiritual fog much of the time. So Benner's words struck home to my heart. But how was I to begin to repractice God's presence?

It was time to take Wrangler for a walk. He is usually eager to bound out, but this morning he kept very close step with me. For several weeks we had been going to dog training and together learning that when I say "with me" he is to stay right by me and not strain ahead. He is so strong and eager; it had not been easy to learn.

But that's exactly what he was doing. When we got to a favorite woodsy area and sat down on a bridge in the sun, he sat as close to me as he could and put his head on my lap. I remembered how he had done the same thing when we got up.

Wrangler wanted to be *with me*—just to be together in the sun and quiet of that cold Sunday morning. When we walked, I didn't have to hold him back. When I sat, he sat. There were no words at first, just the warm feeling of each other's company and the sense that we belonged together.

As Wrangler and I sat on the bridge, I prayed over and over, "Be still and know that I am God." Wrangler listened attentively to my voice.

That was when I realized that Wrangler Blue Dog had been my spiritual director, at least for the day. He did not tell me what I had to do. He just showed me by his actions, without a word. It was as if the Lord had told him, "Wrangler, show that friend of yours that he doesn't have to make some great effort or practice some heroic discipline. All he has to do is be with me and soak in my Word and my presence. I just want him to stay with me."

Wrangler is not yet listed on a website of available spiritual directors. But perhaps he should be.

Postscript. I have to report that the next week Wrangler tried to eat the cat and ended up with a mouthful of golden hair. Which remind us that even spiritual directors can backslide.

5

Active Life
A Slower Pace in a Faster World

We live in an age of continuous partial attention.
LINDA STONE

Ruthlessly eliminate hurry.
DALLAS WILLARD TO JOHN ORTBERG

Only one thing is needed.
JESUS

Terce is the marker of midmorning. It was at this "third hour" on the day of Pentecost that the Spirit came to the early Christian community, as the enabling Power of their witness. In the monastery Terce is time to take a break from busy work, time to receive a midmorning blessing with a focus on the Holy Spirit and the aliveness of his presence.

In terms of our life cycle, we might think of Terce as the time of extending our active life. For Jeanie and me these were the years of starting a ministry and a family. Responsibilities were increasing, and so were the pressures—long periods of travel for me, for Jeanie at home with three children much of the time. These were fulfilling—and frazzled—years.

As a spiritual life stage, this may be our "sent" time. As in the fullness of time Jesus was sent into the world on the Father's mission (Gal 4:4), so we are discovering our mission and becoming more and more involved in job, church, community.

A PUTTING-OFF MORNING

After a writing hiatus of some weeks, this morning I'd decided that after breakfast I would give my first attention (having already had time to pray, stretch and walk) to writing about distractedness.

But then I found myself falling into the same old habit, doing anything else—opening up some e-mails, signing letters, listening to voicemail messages, calling to get an address, shuffling through some bills to be paid—except getting down to the priority of the morning.

At lunch I told my young assistant how distracted I had been. He laughed and said, "I went home the other day and found my roommate cleaning our apartment. And since we don't often clean up, especially deep cleaning, I asked him, 'Don't you have a paper due tomorrow?' And I was right—he did have a paper to write and was putting off starting any way he could."

Why are we so easily distracted?

My first inclination is to blame the noisy and busy world around us. Then I realize it is far more my distractible self that is the problem.

On a recent Christmas Day our small granddaughter Anabel went from one exciting new toy to another, never staying long with any one. Soon she was so frustrated and out of sorts that she was enjoying nothing to the full! I am like Anabel—except in my case it is not so much the new diversions to enjoy as the really important things to explore that I miss out on. Why is it that so often I let the "many things" of a busy life pull me away from the "main thing" that I should be paying attention to (Lk 10:41-42)?

Distraction has an interesting pedigree. The word comes from the Latin *distractus*, literally meaning to draw or pull apart. It can have a very innocuous sense: a distraction can be an amusement or diversion that relaxes us. But more seriously a distraction is a pull away from what deep down we know is our most fundamental goal, purpose or direction. When we are distracted, we are often confused by conflicting emotions or worries. In the most extreme case a distracted mind is a deranged mind. Those who suffer from schizophrenia have great difficulty in filtering out all the sensory input that swirls around them, and so they struggle to grasp reality.

The more "noise" that surrounds us, the more we absorb, the more likely we are to be distractible, our attention readily diverted and restless, and the more vulnerable we become to all the distractions around.

OUR DISTRACTING WORLD

"In a world where there is a wealth of information, there is often a poverty of attention." So said Ken Mehlman, George W. Bush's presidential campaign manager, about why both the Republican and Democratic political campaigns of 2004 went back to one-doorbell-one-voter strategies. The public, he explained, is so bombarded with media messages of every sort that attention spans are shorter and shorter. So while the campaigns continued to spend huge amounts on media ads, they also recognized they faced "a poverty of attention." The only way to combat it was to add a much more interpersonal dimension — sending volunteers door to door to deliver the message and get out the vote.

"A face-to-face communication," said Mehlman, "is most often the most credible and effective way to reach somebody."

What the politicians have learned certainly applies to all of our lives: more information rushing at us does not mean that we gain more understanding; it can simply make it more difficult for us to pay attention to anything.

But how is it possible *not* to pay attention today? Events rush at us and are communicated at warp speed—24/7 as we say, which is a shorthand way of saying "all the time." All the media—radio, TV, Internet, advertising—go for our attention. They grab at us, suck at us, sidle up next to us, get in our face or our ears, slip in subliminally, tickle our funny bone, work on our guilt, latch on to our neuroses, raise our anxiety level about wrinkles on our faces or terrorists in our cities.

Is there any way *not* to pay attention?

"CONTINUOUS PARTIAL ATTENTION"

The problem in part is that we are usually in a state of overload, living in what Microsoft researcher Linda Stone has called a state of "continuous partial attention."

New York Times columnist Thomas Friedman quoted Stone in a piece on the Davos World Economic Forum. Each attendee received a pocket-sized PC to communicate with other participants. Friedman fumbled around trying to make his work; he said he had so many devices he needed someone just to carry them around for him.

Continuous partial attention, Friedman wrote, "means that while you are answering your e-mail and talking to your kid, your cell phone rings and you have a conversation. You are now involved in a continuous flow of interactions in which you can only partially concentrate on each. . . . You're never out anymore. The assumption now is that you're always in. . . . And when you are always in, you are always on. And when you are always on, what are you most like? A computer server."

As Linda Stone put it, "If being fulfilled is about committing yourself to someone else, or some experience, that requires a level of sustained attention," we are in trouble, since sustained attention is just the skill we are losing.

In his bestselling *The Lexus and the Olive Tree*, Friedman observes that the way we measure things has changed. In the era of the Cold War the "weight" of missiles was a defining factor. In our globalized world it is speed that makes the difference. The question then was "How big is your missile?" The question now is "How fast is your modem?" Add the ever-accelerating speed and pace of life to our wired world, and we have the perfect formula to produce — or better seduce — distractible people.

At another session of the Davos conference, corporate life was described as going faster and faster with less time for family, friendship, play. "This sounds like a description of hell!" burst out the chairman of Sony America.

Our highly organized religious lives don't always help. The typical midsized to large North American church is densely programmed. One potential member said to a minister friend of mine, "Pastor, after looking at all the scheduled activities for this week I don't think I'm physically fit to join your church!" He was only half-joking.

For some years the trend among growing "seeker-friendly" churches has been to offer "full-service" religious programming, one-stop opportunities for every age group and every family member (or every single), with lots of parking. Yet while these programs undoubtedly help many people, I wonder if there may not be a deep and quiet counter-movement, a search for places that offer a space for silence, where people can say, "I can come and be quiet here."

A teacher friend, who is busy lecturing at seminary all week and preaches most Sundays at growing evangelical churches, tells me that early each Sunday morning he has begun going to an Anglican church down the road. There he can quiet his soul in the silence before venturing into the busyness of the "day of rest!"

Friedman observes that technological change and instant communication have created two worlds: the "Fast World" and the "Slow World," shaped by the varied responses to globalization. Perhaps in a faster world we could use a slower church — or at least churches that help us to slow down and pay attention.

Not long ago I visited Berlin and stood at the place where the Berlin Wall once divided East Berlin from the West. My mind went back to the mid-1960s, when I stood with a group of friends and looked across Checkpoint Charlie to the grim-looking Eastern sector, where VOPO guards stood with guns at the ready. Although we were there for a world Christian conference, I must confess that our talk that day was more about politics than about faith.

Several times in subsequent years I had traveled to the old East Berlin to spend time with Christian leaders and friends, some of whom had been imprisoned for their active witness to their faith. My memories are of squat, unimaginative buildings, gaunt faces and gray streets and a sense of foreboding, a kind of "looking-over-your-shoulder-to-see-if-big-brother-is-watching" feeling. What shops were open had precious little to offer (except for the "hard currency" shops on the top of certain buildings, where diplomats and the favored few could buy Western goods and appliances if they had cash).

Berlin today is a totally different city. On this recent visit our first-class hotel was in the old East Berlin, surrounded now by all kinds of "lifestyle" shops. Around the corner was a Subway sandwich place and nearby a Banana Republic. A line down the middle of the street is the only reminder of the Wall, although crosses still mark spots where escapees from the East had been shot down. I remembered the scenes of delirious celebration in 1989 when the Wall came down and crowds took away stone after stone when "freedom" came.

But while the symbol of the Wall has been replaced by the Web, our world is still divided: between the "Fast World" of the Web and the "Slow World" that still uses age-old patterns of communication. And those of us in the Fast World can perhaps learn through the ways of peoples in the Slow World.

Bruce Chatwin, the British travel writer, had a learning experience in the "slow world" of the Australian outback. He gave a ride in his Land Cruiser to an aboriginal friend who was on a pilgrimage back to the landscapes of his youth, trying to rediscover the meaning of his own life. Chatwin drove down the dirt road at what seemed to him the leisurely speed of twenty-five miles an hour. But his aboriginal friend jumped around from one window to the other, almost frantic, singing out the names of the places he was seeing and trying to remember.

It suddenly dawned on Chatwin that he was out of tune, going at the wrong speed. So he slowed the vehicle down to the four-mile-an-hour pace that a person would walk. Thus the song of the man, the speed of the ride and the recovery of his spirit could match. The aboriginal knew in his soul what Chatwin learned: there is a connection between our speed and the health of our spirit.

A LITTLE STORY ABOUT ATTENTIVENESS

Jesus often visited a certain small village for a time of retreat and rest. His close friends there, the sisters Mary and Martha and their brother Lazarus, had the gift of making their house a respite for their weary friend, away from the needy crowds that pressed in on him constantly.

On one occasion Martha welcomed him, as Luke puts it (Lk 10:38-42), into "her" home. While her sister and brother also lived there, the place was regarded as "hers"—a tiny clue to possessiveness and how much being in charge must have meant to her.

When Jesus came in, Mary chose to sit at his feet and listen to what he had to say. Perhaps he spoke of his recent travels and rehearsed to them the teachings he had given to his disciples.

Meanwhile Martha was going about her tasks as mistress of the house and fixing a meal. After a time, distracted by her many tasks, she came to Jesus, clearly resenting that Mary was not pitching in, and gave vent to her frustration.

"Lord, do you not care that my sister has left me to do all the work by myself? Tell her then to help me." As if to say, you talk a lot about love and kindness, but what good is that if we don't practice it? And what kind of follower is Mary if she doesn't put her faith to work?

Jesus' answer is practical on one level, profound on another. Not for a moment does he discount the good and necessary work Martha is doing or suggest that the mundane tasks of everyday don't matter. But gently, ever so gently, he chides her: "Martha, dear Martha. You are worried and distracted by many things."

Note his choice of words: "worried and distracted." This good woman, intent on serving Jesus and her other guests well, was anxious and worried, "pulled apart" (the root meaning of *worried*). That is what worry and distraction do: split us down the middle, divide us against ourselves.

It was not so much the multitasking that was churning her up as that in trying to do so many things she was letting herself be torn up.

"Only one thing is needed," Jesus continued. Perhaps he was saying, "Don't worry about a huge meal. Just fix something simple." But his words also clearly carry a deeper meaning: "There is need of only one thing. Mary has chosen the better part, which will not be taken away from her."

The *good*—in this case cleaning the house and cooking the meal—was keeping Martha from the *best:* enjoying the present moment and the all-too-rare presence of their great friend.

Even more deeply, what Mary had chosen and what Martha was missing was the kind of attentive listening for the word that would speak to their hearts' deepest longings and bring into their household routine a visitation of the eternal.

In centuries to come in the life of the church, these two sisters would become symbols for two different "orders" or styles of piety. Martha would be the patron of those called to the "active" life of a vocation in the world. Mary would be the model of those who, isolated from secular affairs, would devote themselves to the "contemplative" life. Like her they would spend their lives sitting figuratively (and truly) at the feet of Jesus.

Here is a truth to consider and practice: some are called more to the "mundane" and others more to the "spiritual" side of things, and we can respect those differences. But it seems to me that this story is teaching something more: that we *all* have "Martha" and "Mary" parts in us, and we all are called to pay attention both to action and to contemplation.

As Mother Teresa explained about the work of her Sisters of Mercy in caring for the dying poor, "Do not think of us as social workers. We are contemplatives in the midst of life. We pray the work."

This is the kind of attention Jesus desired from both Martha and Mary (and for us). That seems clear in the way Luke introduces this story. But why does he tuck this little incident in where he does?

A quick look at the setting (Lk 10–11) shows us it is a kind of "hinge" happening. Immediately before this story Jesus sends the disciples out to tell the message of the kingdom far and wide, to prepare the way in every village where he was headed, and to do it with urgency. It was an important and a consuming task, and they returned fulfilled but weary. Then in answer to a question about

what are the greatest command-
ments, he tells the story of the good
Samaritan, who comes across and
cares for the victim of a beating and
robbery on a deserted road. It is a
picture of busy, hectic, caring, ex-
hausting activity.

Then comes the Martha and
Mary story. And immediately after
Jesus' disciples, probably a bit overwhelmed with their new responsibilities, ask him to teach them to
pray.

He teaches them the words of
what we call the Lord's Prayer and
then says to them,

> Suppose one of you has a
> friend, and you go to him at
> midnight and say to him,
> "Friend, lend me three loaves
> of bread; for a friend of mine
> has arrived, and I have noth-
> ing to set before him." And he
> answers from within, "Do not
> bother me; the door has al-
> ready been locked, and my
> children are with me in bed; I
> cannot get up and give you
> anything." I tell you, even
> though he will not get up and
> give him anything because he

A SUNDAY ON THE ELBE

All day we moved,
or rather
we were moved.

We were current,
were with the flow.
And . . . we were observed.

Some cows, unblinking,
	incurious,
watched us go by.
A swan, imperially white,
disdainful, swam.
The hyper little dog
pumped its legs and barked
to come on board,
while ghosts, from loves
	and wars
no longer current,
peered dumbly down from
high and empty castles.

So we were moved,
and we were seen.

But were we moved . . . to see?

As at each bend the hills
closed ranks behind us
while up ahead new landscapes
lay in waiting
not looked upon,
but were they yet unknown?

By evening, when we came
	to rest,

along the little town
the edges of the dark crept
  down the hills,
a curtain closed across the
  windows of the day.

A half-lit spire gestured up
to draw our eyes,
to pull our hearts
to where a solitary shining
star bemused the sky.

One still point
in a changing day.

BAD SCHANDAU, GERMANY
JUNE 6, 2004

is his friend, at least because
of his persistence he will get
up and give him whatever he
needs. (Lk 11:5-8)

Jesus is not saying that God is
like the sleepy friend. He is teaching by contrast that it is because
God *does* pay attention that his disciples should keep on asking, and
it will be given to them.

*Jesus is calling me to a double atten-
tion:* attention to those around me
in need, as the good Samaritan
cares for the beaten traveler, and
attention to the God who alone
can supply the resources I need to respond well when some weary
and hungry traveler unexpectedly knocks at my door.

A STORY FOR OUR BUSY LIVES

The story of Martha and Mary is one for you and me, for we too
are often distracted, pulled apart by the multiplying choices of our
world, tensed by the pace of change.

Hurry is the great enemy of the life of the spirit. Once when I was
talking with some executives and their spouses about priorities and
sorting out the important from the urgent, a Monsanto executive said
with a rueful laugh, "I spent most of last year on planes, visiting our
plants around the world. At the end of the year I added up all my flight
times, related that to the air speed of the planes I was on and the number of hours in a year, and realized my body speed had averaged about
forty-five miles per hour for the year. I have little time to slow down."

I suppose that most of us live more like tourists rushing to keep up with an itinerary than pilgrims drinking in the lands we are passing through. We all, clergy and laity, get chewed up and distracted. Most of us, if we are honest, are latter-day Marthas who deep inside are longing for some Mary time.

And what is the secret to living in such a world and time? Jesus' words tell us the secret is not *at the circumference* (merely reducing our activities) but *at the center* (refocusing our heart).

Linger for a while on those words of Jesus: *Only one thing is needful.*

Let them lead you to the quiet voice that says to you, as it did to Martha: one thing is necessary. And like Mary, choose what is best.

WHY IS "ONLY ONE THING" NEEDFUL?

The answer, clearly, is that if we do not pay attention, we will not see. We will miss the most important things, as Martha was close to doing.

"The heart," says Blaise Pascal, "has reasons that reason knows nothing of."

And if the imagination of our heart is to be clear and pure, then we must allow space and time for the eyes of our heart to see through, under and beyond appearances, to answer the lure of the deep.

Depth speaks to depth. Deep things open themselves to deep places of the heart. I do not have in mind occult beliefs and practices, mysteries available only to certain initiated ones. Rather I refer to the mystery of how God has made us. In the words of Paul: "The Spirit searches all things, even the deep things of God. For who among men knows the thoughts of a man except the man's spirit within him? In the same way no one knows the thoughts of God except the Spirit of God" (1 Cor 2:10-11 NIV).

The God who has created us with depths that nothing in this world can satisfy, says Paul, has also revealed to us by his Spirit what "no eye has seen, no ear has heard, no mind has conceived," that is, "what God has prepared for those who love him" (1 Cor 2:9-10).

It is just because of these depths of God's love for us and the eternal longing he has created in us that God calls us to be attentive to the many-colored splendor of graces that he lavishes on us. Attentiveness is much more than our attempt to see and understand; it is a species of faith, an open and receptive trust that God has much to reveal to us when we pay attention.

Some things reveal themselves, yield themselves, only to attentive waiting.

This is true of great painting, great music and literature. There are formula novels that we read once and are entertained and totally forget. There are great books, on the other hand, that speak to us so profoundly that we can come back to them again and again, and with each reading, at a new time of our life, we understand ourselves and our world more powerfully. One of my friends, for example, has read most of Faulkner's works dozens of times.

This is especially true of poetry. Another friend has read William Wordsworth's "Ode: Intimations of Immortality" at least fifty times, and each time is left in deeper wonder.

Great paintings likewise give themselves only to those who pause and gaze without haste. Juliet Benner has written,

Spirituality is all about seeing. It is becoming aware of realities in which we are immersed but of which we are unaware. . . . Spiritual vision requires learning to notice the presence of God within and around us. The Christian tradition provides many ways to do this. . . . Much of the classical art in our modern museums was originally created for this spiritual purpose. They still speak profoundly to our souls if we are willing to sit before them and open ourselves to the Scriptures that were their inspiration.

Yet, Benner notes, according to statistics from art galleries, the average visitor spends only three seconds looking at a work of art.

How many times have we heard someone say about another who is deeply in love, "I don't know what he sees in her." Of course we can't see as the lover sees. We have not taken the time to look deeply into that other person's eyes, to listen to their thoughts, to explore their heart. The lover sees, not perfectly of course, with vision distorted no doubt by the lover's own projected needs, but still truly discerns the deep things of the beloved. We may laugh indulgently at puppy love, but it is real to the puppy, and over time it can grow to be something truly visionary.

How deeply do we look at nature? Larry McMurtry, known for his *Lonesome Dove*, wrote another book about roads—the many roads he had driven on and the hundreds of miles he had explored across America. At last, returning in memory to the place where he grew up in east Texas, he recalls that his father had seldom gone much farther than the dusty roads near his dirt farm. Comparing his own travels to his father's localized life, McMurtry admits, "I have looked at many places quickly. My father looked at one place deeply."

In all likelihood McMurtry's father never heard of the Jesuit poet Gerard Manley Hopkins or read his work. But my guess is he would have understood what Hopkins called the *inscape* of things—the deep reality of creation known only to attentive eyes and hearts in the landscapes around.

So in all of life there is the rule:

The things that don't matter can be regarded with indifference and forgotten.

The good things of life take priority.

But the best and deepest are discovered only through attentive waiting.

Only one thing is needful.

Practicing Attentiveness: Reading for Transformation

How do we approach the reading of Scripture? Somehow when I was much younger I thought the ideal was to read as much as possible of the Bible. Indeed it is important for us to know the entire corpus of the Bible, not just favorite bits and pieces. We need to understand the great sweep of the Story of God and how our story with its small *s* relates to God's Story. Still, I am now beginning to slow down and realize that the Scriptures yield their most precious and life-changing truths only to attentive reading.

Metropolitan Anthony Bloom writes of attentive reading:

> Often we consider one or two points and jump to the next, which is wrong, since . . . it takes a long time to become recollected, what the Fathers call an attentive person, someone capable of paying attention to an idea so long and so well that nothing of it is lost. The spiritual writers of the past and of the present day will all tell us: take a text, ponder on it hour after hour, day after day, until you have exhausted all your possibilities, intellectual and emotional, and thanks to attentive reading and re-reading of this text, you have come to a new attitude.

This is the kind of reading that brings not just information but transformation.

One Who Paid Attention
Kierkegaard's Lanterns, Fireworks and Stars

IN THE CENTURY BEFORE THERE WERE Land Cruisers that could go twenty-five miles an hour in the Australian outback (or spacecraft that could fly at supersonic speeds), the Danish philosopher Søren Kierkegaard wrote two small parables that illuminate our human condition of speed and inattention.

A certain rich man traveled in a finely appointed carriage, with lanterns on each corner of his vehicle to light the road around and ahead. He went his way in satisfaction and security, assured that his wealth provided him with a good life. One day along the road the rich man passed a poor peasant who had no carriage to carry him, no lamp to light his way. Yet while the rich man pitied the poor peasant who had no money to buy all the creature comforts, the poor peasant could see the stars, which the rich man missed because he was blinded by his lamps.

Another Kierkegaard parable compared fireworks to the stars. Displays of fireworks hold our attention with increasing levels of dazzlement. They start at a modest pace, then become louder, with more and more rockets exploding in multiple directions, showering more brilliant colors, going ever higher into the night sky, until with one final burst of noise and brilliance and color it is all over. The creators of firework shows, said Kierkegaard, have to produce more and more artificial excitement to keep us entertained, but with the stars it is far different. We can, if we will, lie on our back on a hill gazing into the night sky, hour after hour, and always there is more to see in the unchanging canopy of the stars overhead, more almost magical attraction, more sensing the mystery of the stars whose message in light was sent to us from millions of years past, more drawing of our souls to consider the vastness of eternity and the meaning of time.

Stars are like messengers sent by the Creator who also made *us*, to lure us into pondering the meaning of it all and to consider the great end of our lives. Fireworks are like the diversions *we* create to keep us from facing the reality of our lives.

But what is it in me that blinds me to their signals? That chooses not to slow down? That prefers fireworks displays to stargazing?

6 The Noonday Demon
Our Distractible Selves

*The opportunity which God sends does not
wake up him who is sleeping.*
SENEGALESE PROVERB

Distracted from distraction by distraction.
T. S. ELIOT

The destruction that wastes at noonday.
PSALM 91:6

High noon in the course of hours is called Sext. In the monastery it is a break from work to eat and serve and pray together and to listen as someone reads out loud. It is, as Steindl-Rast says, "the hour of fervor and commitment, but it is also the hour of temptation to laziness and despair: the hour of the noonday devil as well as of intensity."

Deborah Smith Douglas writes, "We are often susceptible in the middle of our days to the subtle wiles of the noonday demon." We can think of high noon not only as the middle of the day but also as the midpoint of our life, or the halfway marker of our college days, or our family life, or a particular vocation or project, when life weighs us down.

Distraction is not always a bane. It can be a blessing when distractions are "divine interruptions" by which God gets our attention to turn us in a new direction.

If we have an active and curious mind, we may well tend to be aware of what is going on at the edges of our attention. Howard Gardner, a Harvard educator, has popularized the concept of "multiple intelligences," that the human brain is capable of many kinds of learning—verbal, emotional, mathematical and so forth—and that a young person who does not do well on tests of verbal or mathematical aptitude may in fact have great potential in relationships or the visual arts. So the healthy mind (and soul) ought to be able to refocus attention over and over in various directions.

To be able to pay active attention to distractions and to learn from them is not a weakness but a strength. In fact many of our most important discoveries about life, the world and ourselves may come from those moments of interruption when our attention is called away to something brand new.

Sir James Simpson, the Scottish scientist whose discovery of the anesthetic use of chloroform saved millions from unbearable pain, celebrated in poetic praise the unexpected insight that caught his attention and led to the discovery.

This day, relenting, God hath placed within my hand a wondrous thing. And God be praised!

His discovery was a gift that came through but also from outside his own thought patterns. So, as with this great scientist, life-transforming discoveries can arise from the interruptions that come our way.

Think of the many characters in the Bible whose lives are changed by paying attention to a "divine interruption"—for example:

- Moses, tending sheep in the desert, suddenly sees a bush burning yet not burned up.
- Jacob, on his way to meet his estranged brother, encounters a mysterious "wrestler" in the night

- The fanatical Saul, on his mean-spirited journey to Damascus to hassle and arrest followers of Jesus, has the same Jesus appear to him in a blinding light.

Each of their lives takes on breathtaking new meaning, a new call — Moses to lead God's people out of captivity in Egypt, Jacob to become the first to be named "Israel," Paul to become the apostle to the nations — because they paid attention to a divine distraction. Similarly of course there is Mary, the mother of Jesus, whose marriage plans were turned upside down when an angel announced that the holy Son of God was being formed in her.

Think what the world would have missed if any of these had not been divinely interrupted. Such grace-giving distractions deserve our full attention. And woe to us if we miss them.

STILL BORN

But what if Mary
troubled by the angel's
pregnant words,
flinching from the Spirit's
shadowed touch
had weighed the odds,
felt the seducing weight
of the conventional way
and said,
"No"?

Or if Joseph
concerned for appearances
protective of his fiancée's
reputation
(and his own)
had listened to his common sense
and quietly broken
the engagement?

Would not the Child
still have been born
for the world?

But what would have been
still-born
in them?

SPIRITUAL ATTENTION DEFICIT DISORDER

This kind of illuminating distraction, however, is very different from the distractibility that diverts me from my true vocation, bending my attention away from what I know I am called to do and be.

Why am I so easily seduced by the flash and flurry of the world around? What is it within me that wants to keep up the fast pace? That seems even to welcome the distractions?

Someone has suggested that we suffer from SADD—a kind of spiritual attention deficit disorder, a deficit I know well.

As I write this morning, I am at our daughter's place in the North Carolina Blue Ridge Mountains. There is a lovely view from here across a lake and up to Grandfather Mountain, a princely height whose profile resembles a grandfatherly face at rest.

But as I took my usual morning walk, a thick cloud cover hid "Grandfather" from my sight, and I was reminded of how Denise Levertov described her morning walks near Mount Rainier:

Sometimes the mountain
is hidden from me in veils
of cloud, sometimes
I am hidden from the mountain
in veils of inattention, apathy, fatigue,
when I forget or refuse to go
down to the shore or a few yards
up the road, on a clear day,
to reconfirm
the witnessing presence.

Like Levertov, I too become tangled in veils that make me forget or refuse to lift up my eyes to the hills and remember the God of my life. I am often blinded to the "witnessing presence" by veils she mentions and my own "veils" woven out of spiritual disarray.

THE VEILS OF SPIRITUAL DISARRAY

Sheer fatigue is one veil. Someone has said that the world is run by tired people. It is a scary thought that decisions at the highest levels of our nations and businesses, our schools and churches, are made by people whose judgment is often clouded by fatigue. The weariness comes not just from the many demands leaders face in their jobs but from the constant, demanding, draining drumbeat of their inner voices.

Psychologist Archibald Hart has written about the way in which stress (whether good stress or bad) increases our adrenaline flow. Many young leaders especially, he says, mistake the adrenaline highs they get through involvement in high-demand ministry for the presence of the Holy Spirit! Then when adrenaline runs down and leaves them utterly exhausted, they wonder what they have done wrong.

I read that and say "ouch!" Hart's pointed words apply as much to me as to my younger friends. In fact the older I get the more my racehorse brain seems to urge me on: "Keep going! Don't stop! Remember all you have to do!" Until my aging body and mind call out, "Enough already! Who do you think you are, God? Even God rested on the seventh day!"

When I finally do stop, or am stopped, I realize how much is going on right now, how much I am missing because my tired brain has been too weary even to stop, look and take in.

(I stop writing here and pause for a moment to stand and look up: ah, the cloud is beginning to lift off Grandfather!)

Another veil that kept Levertov from witnessing her mountain was apathy: the "I don't care" attitude that comes not just from physical or mental fatigue but from a soul-weariness, rooted either in a profound wound or in sheer frustration with life and the world.

Jason Read, selected as "stroke," or pacesetter, on the U.S. Olympic rowing team in 2004, is a case study in the first: the profound indifference produced by tragedy. Following the 2001 attacks on the World Trade Center, Read lost his taste not only for rowing but for everything. As chief of a rescue squad, he helped to coordinate operations at Ground Zero for five days. What he experienced, he said, was enough to give a normal person a lifetime of nightmares, and he recalls having "a sense of apathy about all things in the world that had meant so much to me. Did I want to row anymore? Did I want to be chief of a volunteer rescue squad? What did it mean? All those people had been killed. Game over. Mortality became reality in a matter of seconds." Coming out of apathy was hard; it took not only a recommitment to rowing but an even deeper rediscovery of his faith.

The day after he came back from Ground Zero, he attended worship at his university's chapel: "It was emotional and revitalizing. I prayed very hard—for the first time in my life." With the support of his friends and the counsel of the rowing team chaplain, and building on his own ability to be optimistic even in the midst of ugliness and tumult, he was back three years later not only as a superb athlete but also as a man renewed and grateful for each and every moment of life.

Read's experience is dramatic, but just as often apathy has its root in the frustrations of ordinary, everyday life.

The church fathers spoke of apathy as *acedia*—a state of soul marked by sluggishness, moodiness and distaste for spiritual things. Acedia is a loss of motivation for doing spiritual work.

Most strikingly, the fourth-century monk John Cassian called acedia "the noonday demon." He pictured a monk in the desert, sitting in his cell at high noon, sleepy, tired, unable to concentrate, sick of trying to pray—and dreaming of leaving the monastery and running off, as we would say, to do his own thing.

Thomas Aquinas thought of acedia as having its root not in laziness but in sadness: a sorrow that makes us flee from the very love and joy that God has for us.

A contemporary writer, Deborah Smith Douglas, describes acedia as a "sin of the long haul"—the temptation that comes in the middle of our days, when we are worn out by the long, long journey through a wilderness that seems to have no end. "None of us," she writes, "is immune to its dangers. As we move deeper into the middle of our days, the middle of our lives, it becomes ever more important to stay awake, to remain faithful."

And what is the antidote to acedia and apathy, according to the ancient writers? Exactly what Jason Read found: to do the opposite of what we feel and to recommit ourselves to attend to the job at hand (including physical work), to prayer and to humility.

Anxiety also veils my attention. I sometimes imagine that Jesus must surely have looked out and seen my own anxious face in the crowd when he gave his Sermon on the Mount, and that he had me (and you!) in mind when he gently chided our distracted, anxious preoccupation with ourselves: "Do not worry about your life. . . . Who of you by worrying can add a single hour to his life? . . . Therefore do not worry about tomorrow, for tomorrow will worry about itself" (Mt 6:25, 27, 34 NIV). Instead, he instructed, "Give your entire attention to what God is doing right now, and don't get worked up about what may or may not happen tomorrow" (Mt 6:34 *The Message*).

How often I wake up in the morning and my inner voice begins to worry me with overnight messages stored in my personal "mailbox" during the hours of sleep. Sometimes these morning messages are welcome solutions—overnight my subconscious has worked out answers to puzzles I'd had to put on hold. But just as often I wake up feeling as if a thousand wild horses are demanding attention, pulling at me insistently: *You need to call* _____. *You must write* _____. *You have to* _____. *Don't forget to* _____. *What will happen if* _____? (Why is it that the wild horses stomp the loudest if I wake up at 4 or 5 a.m.?)

Usually these anxious thoughts are leftovers from the night before, unfinished business that I have forgotten to leave in God's
hands, where it belongs anyway. And if I do not turn them over to
him by high noon, my mind is in a worse state.

I have resolved over and over to let my first thought in the morning be of God: to still and quiet my soul, "like a weaned child with
its mother" (Ps 131:2 NIV), to be still and know that he is God. But
again and again, like Levertov, I

> forget or refuse to go
> down to the shore or a few yards
> up the road, on a clear day,
> to reconfirm
> the witnessing presence.

Why? Why do I forget or refuse? Do I still think that by worrying
I can add hours to my life?

A "spirit of fear" is yet another veil, stealing away attentiveness.
If anxiety is a kind of free-floating worry about life in general, fears
can be very specific. A fear reaction to physical danger constricts
the vision and makes it difficult for us to see the way out. Spiritual
fear can constrict our vision of the way God has in mind for us.

No wonder that Paul, writing to his young, gifted, dedicated but
somewhat timid protégé Timothy, reminded him that "God did not
give us a spirit of timidity, but a spirit of power, of love and of self-
discipline" (2 Tim 1:7 NIV).

Fears come in all shapes and sizes. The fear of failure—or perhaps more truly the fear of not living up to all I want to be, or of
not living up to all my mother Ford expected me to be, always a little "better than others"—lurked around me for some years and still
sometimes stares over my shoulder.

If I put off starting to write, it is often because that ghost of "being better" is whispering: *What if nothing comes? Or if I write and*

no one reads it? What if I can't be funny, or moving, or fresh, or original? What if what I write is just—ordinary, average? Over the last decade or so I have learned to love painting in watercolors and pastels. But the same unfriendly ghost sometimes shows up muttering that my next painting may not be good at all, *so why start?*

The paradox is that the less I prepare, the more freely I allow myself to speak, or write, or paint . . . or dance . . . or love, the better it seems to be. It's scary—but it's real. It's as if God replaces the spirit of fear with a joyful sense of who he has made me to be.

Not all the "veils" are so serious, of course. Sometimes simple absent-mindedness makes me "forget to go down to the shore"— just as I forget where I left my keys or glasses, or turn on the alarm system inadvertently. That kind of inattention I hope I can laugh about and forget.

THE ROOT OF INATTENTION

There is, however, behind most of these veils another deeper root cause of our inattention: the veil of sin.

I use the term *sin* here advisedly, not *sins* plural—the bad things we do—but *sin* singular, the wrong-centeredness of who we are, the profound spiritual dislocation that hides us both from God and from our true selves.

Douglas Steere, the Quaker teacher, writes that prayer consists of attentiveness, and sin is "anything that destroys this attention." At the deepest level, the "veils" that keep us from paying atten-tion—whether the speed and noise of our world, the workaholism that wears us down to the bone, the apathy that shuts off our feel-ings, or the fears that haunt us—all come from our refusal to admit our creatureliness.

Our pastor, who as a teenager had left the church and the faith behind when he went off to college, tells of his conversion at (of all things) a play about Galileo, who was at such odds with the church of his day. "I had gone to the play," he says, "only to get some extra credit for a physics course. But my life was changed that night when I realized: I am not the center of the universe." How hard it is to truly confess that!

We keep on hurrying and staying busy and chattering because we are afraid that if we did slow down, stop working, get still long enough to listen deeply, we might have to face our mortality and humanness and give up trying to run our lives like little gods.

My office is in our home these days. It is a great advantage not to have to get in the car and go some place to work. But it is also a great temptation to give in to the "thinkaholism" my daughter teases me about. My wife Jeanie gets very exasperated when I keep going into the home office at all hours to do one more thing. Finally I bought a sign at a hardware store that says CLOSED on one side and OPEN on the other! The idea was that once the working day should be done I would close the door, put the sign on it and let that be enough. But somehow I seem to be able to find many excuses to ignore the big letters CLOSED and go back to work. It is not a habit I am happy about. I know that when I get so focused on work I am likely missing out on other things—including small things of great significance—that are awaiting my attention.

More than once I have wondered whether I am addicted to work. Psychiatrist Gerald May describes addictions as "attachments," coming from the French word *attaché*, which means to be nailed to something. He believes that we are nailed to our addictions—drugs or alcohol, sex or relationships, work or even our "self-image"—because we refuse or are afraid to admit our need of grace. Because we will not humble ourselves to acknowledge both our humanness and our brokenness, we desperately seek to control our lives, rather than experience the freedom of living as the children of God.

At the end of the day, then, inattentiveness is a control issue: I would rather try to control the trivial than surrender to the Eternal and end up not in control at all. And we refuse to surrender control because we deep down think we have to justify our existence rather than be justified by the free grace of God.

How do we become truly human? By our efforts to become god-like? Or by God's gracious gift of making us his sons and daughters? This is the age-old classic conflict between law and grace, pinpointed by Jesus in his invitation "Come to me, all you who are weary and burdened, and I will give you rest" (Mt 11:28 NIV). It's also the underlying theme of Paul's letters to the early followers of Christ. As he put his concern to the believers in Galatia: "We know that a person is justified not by the works of the law but through faith in Jesus Christ. . . . You were running well; who prevented you from obeying the truth?" (Gal 2:16; 5:7).

World-class runner Harold Abrahams, a friend and rival of Eric Liddell of *Chariots of Fire* fame, explained his desperate attempts to win the hundred-yard Olympic sprint by saying, "I have just ten seconds to justify my existence!"

Whew! I hear that and wonder how long I will keep trying to "justify my existence." How often I have woken up in the morning thinking, *What do I have to do today to prove I deserve my place in the world?* Or even more desperately, *How long do I have to live to justify my existence? What more do I have to accomplish?*

Why do I need to justify my existence in the first place? After all, I didn't create myself. I didn't ask to be born. I didn't choose where I would grow up or what gifts or opportunities I would have. Since God made me, gave me life, and allotted my times and the places where I would live, I certainly don't need to justify my existence to him. I do want to seek him, find him, understand what he wants and live responsibly before him. But my existence is already justified by the very fact of my existence. Just the fact that I am is a sign of God's enduring love.

This morning I read Psalm 107, in which a key phrase is repeated over and over: "His steadfast love endures forever."

The psalmist reflects on the history of God's people—times of wandering in desert places, of sitting in darkness as prisoners, of being sick through sinful ways, of reeling and staggering like drunkards in a sea storm—and how they cried to the Lord and were redeemed. Again and again he says, "Thank the LORD for his steadfast love."

I did that as I walked our dog in the early-morning mist that hung again on the mountain looming near. I thought back to my birth to an unmarried mother and how I could have been tossed aside. Of the mother who adopted me and would not let me go. Of marriage and family with the blessings and the pain that human love brings. Of dark times of loss and misunderstandings. I realized how steadfast God's love has been through it all, as sure as the sun that shines even when morning mists hide it for a while.

Again I had to ask: if God loves like that, why do I not give him full attention—always and at once?

Deep down I know the reason: I still need to trust his love fully and to allow myself to be loved.

The "veils" that swathe me all speak of this. When I am overtired, it is usually because I have tried to do it all myself and not trusted God's strength fully enough. When I am apathetic, I have not trusted his grace enough. When I am anxious, I have not trusted his goodness and power enough. When I am afraid—especially of failure—I have not trusted his love enough.

And somehow I think that if I have not been paying attention, God will be hurt, angry, put out—even pouting!

What God pouts? Not the God I have seen and known in Jesus.

So this morning, rather than launching in to write up my "conclusion," I decided to sit quietly and reflect on "steadfast love."

I picked up a meditation about Julian of Norwich. "Should I read this?" I half mused out loud, and a voice seemed to say "Yes." So I read about that devout and amazing woman who in the fourteenth century had a series of "showings"—revelations of God's mercy and forgiveness—over a period of two days following a near-fatal illness. The central thought of these "showings," writes Robert Llewelyn, is "the constancy of God's love. No power in heaven or on earth—and that includes sin—can stop God loving us."

When we fall into sin, said Julian, it may seem that God is angry with us, but actually we are often projecting our own disappointment onto God. The truth is that God is present with his forgiveness whether we choose to take it or not.

As Llewelyn says, we can pull down the shades and shut out the sun, but we can never turn the sun's light into darkness. When the shades go up, the sun is still shining. And when we turn to God, his all-compassionate love is waiting to stream into our life.

Reading this, I remembered a very dark night when in the wee hours I could not sleep, feeling very unjustly judged by some erstwhile friends, searching my conscience and wondering what I had done to deserve their condemnation. In those dark hours words (by Philip Yancey) came to my mind and heart:

> Grace means there is nothing we can do to make God love us more. . . .
>
> And grace means there is nothing we can do to make God love us less.

Those words opened the curtains of my soul again to let the amazing light of God's love stream in.

That truth goes to the very root of my distractible self. How hard it is to believe and receive this unconditional love of God. How easy it is to build up my defenses against being loved. And how freeing it is to surrender at last to that love.

As I reflect on the "veils" of inattentiveness, it is fascinating to recall that Paul picked the image of the veil to describe the freedom that Christ brings. When Moses came down Mount Sinai after meeting with God and receiving the law, he put a veil over his face. He wore the veil because the people of Israel could not look steadily at his face. They were dazzled by the glory that was shining there, reflected from the brightness of God's very presence.

Even so, says Paul, the law of Moses' era was a fading glory. It could not give life. In contrast, Christ shines with a lasting glory that takes away all veils and brings liberty.

> Whenever anyone turns to the Lord, the veil is taken away. Now the Lord is the Spirit, and where the Spirit of the Lord is, there is freedom. And we, who with unveiled faces all reflect the Lord's glory, are being transformed into his likeness with ever-increasing glory, which comes from the Lord, who is the Spirit. (2 Cor 3:16-18 NIV)

"Whenever anyone turns to the Lord . . ." That phrase speaks so hopefully to me. It speaks of the love of God—attending and ready.

It encourages me not to be distracted. And if I am? Then I can turn and pay attention to him.

When? Whenever. Like right now!

A woman trying to practice centering prayer told Thomas Keating: "I try to keep my mind on God, and to pay attention. But it seems as if I am always being distracted. I must be distracted a thousand times in twenty minutes."

His response to her is a good final word in making peace with our distractibility: "Wonderful." he replied. "You have a thousand opportunities to turn back to God."

Practicing Attentiveness: Eliminating Hurry

After John Ortberg went to Chicago to be a teaching pastor at Willow Creek Community Church, he discovered that he was moving so fast that his spiritual life was going down the drain. Rather desperately he called Dallas Willard—a professor and writer who had been a spiritual mentor—and asked his counsel.

"Ruthlessly eliminate hurry," was Willard's response.

"That's good," said Ortberg, writing it down. "What's next?"

"There isn't anything else," replied Willard.

This advice speaks to me because, like Ortberg, I have always wanted to move quickly and to be in the traffic lane where I guess the light will first turn green.

Those simple words—"ruthlessly eliminate hurry"—have become an important part of my own "rule of life." I often forget them . . . and just as often recall them.

I no longer regard it as a compliment if someone says, "Leighton can do three things at one time." Instead I take it as a rueful reminder: do one thing at a time, slow down, take time to breathe, to pray, to remember what has just happened with gratitude (or regret), to prepare my heart and mind for what comes next instead of rushing ahead with an overstuffed mind.

Jesus never seemed to be in a hurry. Yet at the end of thirty-three short years he could say to his Father, "I have finished the work you gave me to do" (see Jn 17:4).

If I would stop each noon to remind myself to ruthlessly eliminate hurry, perhaps I could listen more attentively to what Jesus is doing through me, and I too could say at the end of the day, I have finished what God wanted me to do today.

One Who Paid Attention
How Mother Teresa Kept Going

IN 1986 I WAS TRAVELING WITH some friends in India. Since we were passing through Calcutta, we wondered whether it might be possible to visit Mother Teresa and her Sisters of Mercy, who ministered to the poor of the city. I wanted to see her both for my own sake and because she had long been one of my wife's heroes.

We thought it might take months to get an appointment, but one phone call was sufficient. Off a busy, dirty street, where children played in sewer water spewing by the roadside, we came to a modest building marked by a simple sign on a brown wood door: "Sisters of Mercy."

We rang a bell and waited. In a moment, one of the sisters welcomed us shyly and asked us to wait in an area curtained off with blue drapes from the rest of the house. Around it were posted inspirational sayings, such as "I am eternally grateful to Jesus."

When Mother Teresa came in, she was smaller than I had expected, a bit less than five feet tall. She wore a blue and white habit and thick glasses and was barefoot, with a large bunion on one foot.

She apologized for keeping us waiting. "I have to fly to Delhi in a little while," she explained. "They have asked me to talk to some rich people about helping the poor. Can you imagine them asking me?"

We talked about the dying poor with whom she and the sisters ministered as they were brought in from the streets of that teeming city to live out their final days. Many lay on pallets near us as we spoke.

"How do you keep going" I asked, "with so much poverty and death and pain all around?"

"We do our work for Jesus and with Jesus and to Jesus," she answered, "and that's what keeps it simple. It's not a matter of praying some times and working others. We pray the work." She also told us how she and the other sisters sought to see Christ in the face of each one they served.

I went away from that brief encounter more than strangely moved.

Years later, at a prayer breakfast in Washington, D.C., I heard her say, "Don't misunderstand our work. We are not social workers. We do social work. But we are contemplatives in the midst of life."

Jeanie has often reminded me of another of Mother Teresa's sayings: "We cannot do great things. We can only do small things with great love."

That love is at the heart of contemplation. To see whomever we meet with the eyes of Christ. To do whatever work we do as the hands of Christ. To be a "contemplative in the midst of life" is the attitude God wants to renew in us every day and every hour of our lives.

Holy Stillness

An Interlude

Old men ought to be explorers
Here or there does not matter.
We must be still and still moving.
T. S. ELIOT

T. S. Eliot's paradoxical turn of phrase—"be still and still moving"—certainly fits me, because of my current phase of life and especially at certain times of the year.

One early January I hit a wall, mentally exhausted, emotionally and physically drained. It was catch-up time after the pressures of prior months, from the death of my wife's brother Melvin in late August through the recurrence of our daughter Debbie's breast cancer, followed by weeks and weeks of anxiety and chemotherapy, along with all the usual demands and opportunities of ministry.

Then came Christmas. We tried to tone down the rush, but even so the season took its toll, bringing both good and bad stress. Our little granddaughter Anabel came for four days with Kevin and her mother Caroline, and brought with her both absolute delight and perpetual motion. There is no need for nuclear power plants when Anabel is around! She generates nonstop energy. Debbie had another chemo treatment the Monday before Christmas, with side effects that hit hardest on Christmas Day, and even though she was able to take part in family gatherings, all were tinged with the awareness of her vulnerability.

With the New Year came the annual retreat of our Sandy Ford Fellows, seminary student leaders who receive scholarships from Sandy's fund and come together once a year. As always, it was a joyous and rewarding time, four and a half days full of conversation and teaching and worship and simply being together. Immediately after that came a board meeting and the dedication of Gordon-Conwell Theological Seminary's new Charlotte building in honor of Jeanie's parents, Frank and Morrow Graham. Jeanie's loving and humorous remarks were the highlight.

By that weekend, though, I was running on fumes. I was supposed to head to Seattle for a board meeting with World Vision. I love World Vision—the vision and the people. But I dreaded the thought of getting on a plane to the West Coast. My mind could barely hold on to another thought.

My body was also showing signs of weariness. After my usual workouts at the Y, my blood pressure registered 84 over 60, the lowest it has ever been.

For Christmas, friends had sent us a CD featuring a song, "Jesus' Blood Never Failed Me Yet." It consisted totally of the raspy voice of a nameless tramp recorded during the making of a film about homeless people on the streets of London near Waterloo Station. The audio engineer had caught their voices, some bawling out drunken ditties, but also the voice of one old man singing over and over about the blood of Jesus. When the engineer took it back to his studios, his fellow workers were moved to silence and even tears.

Years later, a CD was produced and, surprisingly, became a great hit with English listeners, not exactly fans of gospel music. On it the voice of the old man is sometimes barely audible, as other voices and instruments come in and out. But always that rough, quavering voice sings the same words:

> Jesus' blood never failed me yet,
> Never failed me yet,
> Jesus' blood never failed me yet.
> This one thing I know
> For he told me so,
> Jesus' blood never failed me yet
> Never failed me yet . . .

On and on it goes—for an astonishing seventy four minutes!

That Sunday I e-mailed my friend MaryKate who sent it to me:

> Yesterday I listened to the CD *Jesus' Blood Never Failed Me Yet,* and that raspy voice of the old tramp got to me so that I was in tears. I realized it spoke to the "getting old" man inside of me. No doubt this is in part a time of year thing. I find it difficult to concentrate in prayer, and the smallest demand seems more than I want to respond to!

I almost did not go to church that morning; since we were taking a visitor I did go, but I left after the sermon. Jeanie pointed out later that I had worn a suit coat but an odd pair of pants—a sign of sartorial fatigue.

MaryKate e-mailed back, encouraging me to take time without the pressure of being "on deck," allowing for some emotional space and healing activities. At the same time I read the words of Jesus' mother when the wine ran out at the wedding feast: "Do whatever he tells you" (Jn 2:5). Wise words, which said to me, as I wrote in my journal, "Do the ordinary things today. Not to look for the extraordinary things to do, but to sit quietly for a bit, take a walk, read, make a couple of needed calls only, and get my tooth fixed [a cap had broken off]."

Overcoming my overactive conscience, I reluctantly canceled the trip to the West Coast board meeting. And I did take time to sit, to read, to walk, to pray.

In a *Weavings* article I read a quote from Thomas Merton: "As rays of sun do not set fire to anything by themselves, so God does not touch our souls with the fire without Christ." As I walked quietly and sat for a long time by a stream in our neighborhood, I prayed, "May Christ be the magnifying glass through which I see the ordinary today, so that I may have strength to rise above winter moods." Butternut, our cat, had followed me into the woods, and he and I sat on a rock, gazing at the water and bushes, the rocks and sky, "doing nothing well."

I took another cue from Alice Fryling's *The Art of Spiritual Listening* in which she suggests setting aside time to sit with the verse "Be still, and know that I am God" (Ps 46:10), repeating it over and over, leaving off a word or phrase each time. As I did this, spending a minute or two on each phrase, I wrote down impressions that came to my tired mind and heart.

Be still and know that I am **God.**

You are God, I am not. You are Center. Not my moods, my complaints, my busyness. Not my desires—physical, emotional, sexual or spiritual. Transform them into longing for You.

Be still and know that **I am.**

Make me aware of Your being, in my hands, toenails, teeth. Your light in my physical reality. Your time runs through the ticking of the clocks. The world is running on, as I sit, without me. You are as present as—through—beyond—the sun that gives light today to all I see.

Be still and **know.**

I do not have to read to know. To run to the computer to know. To talk on the phone to know. To be at World Vision to know. To talk to a friend to know. Even to scrutinize my Bible to know (there may be times to stop reading the Bible for a time, as a friend said recently). When I am still, my knowing comes not from without but within, or, more truly, what I see and experience *without* is received and illuminated *within*. Until the light of Christ makes me see. For that I need to . . .

Be **still.**

Not to move. "O, in this single hour I live all of myself and do not move. I, the pursued, who madly ran, stand still, stand still, and stop the sun!" (May Sarton). "Peace, be still." "Still, still with Thee." Why is a "still" so named—a *distillery* of essences? Must we be still to be *distilled*, i.e., purified? Be still my soul.

It was when St. Francis lay still behind a convent, ill, eyes unable to see, that he knew and composed his famous canticle to Brother Sun.

Be still, Leighton. I motion to myself with my hands. Stop. Hush. Stay—as I motion "stay" to Cocoa, our grandson's dog. I rein myself in.

The clock strikes. Ten. I listen to each stroke.

Today I discovered I had an extra week. Somehow my mental calendar had dropped next week. My life suddenly is a week longer. So—will I run? Or be still?

Be.

When I find myself
as a being before God
as a physical being in a world irradiated by light
as a moving creature, urged on, but able to say "Whoa"
I am not ruled by urges
as a temporal being, living in the I Am Eternal One
reminded by the clock to live here, now
I can be content
with whatever I have

When I am still, *compulsion* (the busyness that Hilary of Tours called "a blasphemous anxiety to do God's work for him") gives way to *compunction* (being pricked or punctured). That is, God can break through the many layers with which I protect myself, so that I can hear his Word and be poised to listen.

■ ■ ■

Days passed, and I began to listen daily to those words: "Be still, and know that I am God."

"Stopping" during this month was essential. If I had gone on to Seattle and the rest, I would not have slowed down enough to quiet my mind, to listen truly. It was a sabbath time that I needed.

And the difference is clear. When I am on automatic, I "know" many things very partially. In a mindful state, I "know" a few things quite well. In true contemplation, I "know" one thing at a time deeply. And the many things fuse into one thing.

The paradox of our modern world is that we know so much about so many things, about *how* things work, but so little about *who* we are as persons, *why* we are.

We believers are not immune to this dis-ease. We have more and more sources of information about the Bible, theology, ethics, history, psychology and organization—but relatively little time to absorb even a little bit of the information so that it can form and transform us. Still, sometimes in quiet moments, sometimes at a dramatic crossroads, something may happen that makes us stop, look and listen.

THE SECOND JOURNEY

In novels about clergy, Susan Howatch writes of "the second journey." Often her characters are so mesmerized by glittering images of religious success that they lose the sense of who they are called to be, until something stops them in their tracks.

This launching of a "second journey" comes often at the midpoint of life, when our path turns more from the outward to the inward journey, then an integrating of the two, the discovery of what Merton calls a "hidden wholeness" as we begin more and more to become our true selves, to discover the true End of our lives.

In some seasons of our lives, we are more active, more outwardly focused, more driven. Hopefully as we grow older, there are seasons in which we become more reflective, moving from an action mode to a wisdom mode—assuming we have learned some wisdom from our actions, both good and bad.

This shift is normal in the pattern of our aging and maturing. Along with them come those critical moments at various stages on our journeys, those times of earthquake and upheaval, in which we become more attuned to the "still, small voice" of God, and of our own soul.

Most of us need some kind of spiritual jolt to start us on the second journey, to make us stop and listen long enough to pay attention to what God is saying to us.

PAYING ATTENTION TO THE INTERLUDES
These critical interludes may start us on a "second journey." Such stopping and restarting is not a one-time happening but an ongoing process that goes on and on in our lives. The interludes may be dramatic or almost imperceptible.

At the beginning of that year, I was reminded that in perpetual motion I can mistake the flow of my adrenaline for the moving of the Holy Spirit; I can live in the illusion that I am ultimately in control of my destiny and my daily affairs.

Days later, during a snow and ice storm that canceled all plans for two days, I looked back and realized how important it had been to stand still. Now I could ask with fresh intention:

What is Your will today?
You are God.
I hear two clocks ticking. A reminder that in the hours and
minutes of this day You are present—in my time. I live in
Your eternity, and know that "my times are in Your hand."

I can, in Eliot's words, be still *and* still moving on into the fullness of what God has in mind.

When Shadows Come
Darkness Comes Early

Life is always an unfinished symphony.
KARL RAHNER

From noon on, darkness came over the whole land. . . .
And about three o'clock Jesus cried out, . . .
"My God, my God, why have you forsaken me?"
MATTHEW 27:45-46

N*one* (pronounced with a long "o") marks mid- to late-afternoon time, as the sun begins its descent and shadows start to lengthen. "With None," writes David Steindl-Rast, "we encounter the reality that things don't last forever." The lengthening shadows remind us of endings, but as the day wanes we also pay more attention to the things that endure.

Good Friday was widely observed where I grew up in Canada, not only in some churches (although I can't clearly remember Good Friday services in my church) but also in the wider community. Most businesses closed, at least for the afternoon. As I look back, it seems like a far-off time in a strange land, so different from this time and place where Good Friday and Easter are excuses for a holiday or extra shopping—and Maundy Thursday and Holy Saturday are virtually unknown even to many churchgoers.

The skies, at least in my memory, always seemed to cloud over at midafternoon on Good Friday, and my mother would remind me that was the time that Jesus died on the cross. I watched for the clouds to come and would have been surprised if they had not.

Among the monastic hours, None comes at midafternoon and is associated with darkening. When Jesus was on the cross, Luke tells us, "darkness came over the whole land [from noon] until three in the afternoon, while the sun's light failed" (Lk 23:44-45). Then Jesus uttered his cry of dereliction: "My God, my God, why have you forsaken me?"

Soon he breathed, "It is finished." With that he bowed his head and gave up his spirit. It was time to let go.

LETTING GO AND REACHING OUT

My wife and I were among a small group invited by President Lyndon Johnson to tour the White House on the last Sunday of his presidency. The president met us in the cabinet room and then turned us over to an aide. He explained that he had to go to the Rose Garden, where the Marine band was playing a final salute for him.

That evening in our hotel room we watched the ceremony on the late news. I was startled when the announcer stumbled while explaining that the song the band played was named for the river by the LBJ ranch in Texas. "It's the 'Perdenales Waltz,'" he said. "No, sorry, the 'Pedernales' . . . uhhh . . . the 'Padernales' . . ." Confused, he paused, then said, "Oh well, I guess it doesn't matter now!"

My first reaction was *What a gratuitous insult to the office of the presidency, and the man.* Then I thought, *Sic transit gloria.* So quickly the trappings of power go.

That poignant scene stayed with me and came back to mind when I was in my early sixties and thoughts of mortality began to occupy me. I was brought up short when a friend told me, "I don't think you're afraid to die. I think you're afraid to die before you have fully lived." Those words challenged me to a new kind of discernment, to ask, *What must I let go? What should I hold more closely? And to what could I reach out more hopefully?*

We experience the hour of None as a stage when life caves in and losses begin to mount up. We begin to lose some very precious things, and clouds hover over what we have always taken for granted: health, relationships, job. In the spiritual life we may undergo a dark night of the soul. Yet this is also the time when we begin to pay more attention to things that endure, discerning what lasts in the midst of life's changes.

Thoughts of darkness are not usually the most welcome. We prefer the bright and cheery. Kathleen Norris quotes a writer who said, "The true religions of America are optimism and denial." Yet moving out of denial into reality is absolutely essential if we are to take "the second journey."

Jesus came as "the light of the world" so that those who follow him might not walk in darkness. Yet it is the very fact that *the light shines in the darkness* that makes it so luminous. If the darkness into which Jesus went had not been so deep, neither would the light he brought have shone so brightly.

When our college-age son Sandy died at the age of twenty-one during heart surgery, I received a letter from Marcus Loane, then archbishop of Sydney, Australia, in which he quoted words about "the deep darkness where God is." I searched and found them in the Exodus story about Moses' approaching God in the thick darkness at the summit of Mount Sinai (Ex 20:21).

Those words spoke to me deeply then and have stayed with me in the years since. For it has often been during the None hours of life—the times of the deepest darkness—when I was closest to God, even though I could not sense it at the time.

This was not only because God was present in my dark times. When I first read the Exodus passage, I thought it was saying that God came to the darkness where Moses was. But it actually pictures Moses entering *the darkness where God was*—and is! To enter this darkness is to enter into the mystery of God, to venture into the darkness of the unknown, to let go of the little lights that I want desperately to hold on to, and to know God more deeply in darkness, mystery and even near despair.

When Sandy died, my wife Jeanie expressed in a wonderfully deep and simple way her faith, a faith tested not only by the terrible loss of a child but also by some friends' well-meant but totally off-the-mark efforts to explain the unexplainable. "I understand God less," she said, poignantly and honestly, "but I have learned to trust him more."

PAYING ATTENTION TO OUR TEARS

The old spiritual teachers used to say that it is very important to pay attention to our tears. Athanasius prized "the gift of tears" as the outward sign of God's puncturing of our heart. Deborah Smith Douglas recalls hearing a wise priest say that we should be grateful for whatever breaks our heart: "Reflecting on God's promise to write 'upon' our hearts, rather than 'within' them, he suggested that our own hearts are so hard that all God *can* do is write upon the surface (Jeremiah 31:33). It is only when our hearts break, that they break open: then the word of God can enter deeply, like a seed in a harrowed field."

We should *prize* the gift of tears? What a hard saying that is. Yet I concur with Leon Blum: "Man has places in his heart which do not yet exist, and into them enters suffering in order that they may have existence." Looking back, I know there are in me "places of the heart" that have opened to God's presence, or to welcome the hurt of others, places that I might never have explored had it not been for the dark passages I have come through. In a very strange and mysterious way the light shone in and opened up the darkness. So when tears come, instead of avoiding them I am trying to learn to pay attention, to pause and ask: *What makes these tears come?*

I think of Jacob. It was not in the high noon of his prosperity but through his wrestling with a Stranger in the deep darkest night, struggling with his inner demons as well as the threat he feared from his estranged brother Esau, that Jacob became a man with a new heart and a new name — Israel. When morning came, he walked with a limp from that painful encounter, but in the morning also the sun rose on him (Gen 32:31).

For our daughter Debbie, it was a return bout with breast cancer that eventually brought her into a new sense of calling. Shortly after she learned that she had to face five months of aggressive chemo and radiation, she went out on her regular exercise run and wrestled with the turmoil and fears in her spirit. Later she told me that on her run she had seen a "burning bush" plant in bloom by the roadside, and her mind had gone to Moses' burning bush experience when God called him.

"Do you think God has a special call for me?" she asked. "I have been searching for years as to what God has in mind for me. I don't want it to be on committees anymore."

Today the treatments are ended. The cancer seems to be gone. Deb is feeling and looking well and lovely. But most important, I believe she has also found her calling. For years she has loved putting together beautiful designs and colors for interior design. Now she has set up her own small business, has her license and is helping her first client.

I told her recently, "Deb, this is what you have been made to do. I really believe this is God's calling for you. Your love of beauty, your eye for color, your creative instincts—all are being used. This is your vocation. You are 'letting God's glory through,' as the poet Hopkins said we all are called to do."

PASCHAL MYSTERY: THE MISSING MOMENT

In his fine book *The Holy Longing*, Ronald Rolheiser describes spirituality as "what we do with desire"—the fire inside us. He devotes a chapter to "the paschal mystery," explaining that in Christian spirituality "the most central of all mysteries is the paschal one, the mystery of suffering, death, and transformation."

There are many deaths that we die throughout our life, suggests Rolheiser: the death of our youth, of our spiritual and psychological wholeness, our dreams and our honeymoons, even our ideas of God and the church. As Karl Rahner put it, in this life all symphonies are unfinished.

Yet these many deaths, some small, some huge, may be God's way of bringing transformation and new life. In Jesus' words, "Unless a grain of wheat falls to the ground and dies, it remains just a single grain; but if it dies, it bears much fruit" (Jn 12:24).

I find enormously helpful the distinction Rolheiser makes between two kinds of death: *terminal* death, which ends life and possibility, and *paschal* death, which is just as real but opens us to deeper and richer forms of life. The paschal mystery, as Rolheiser describes it, "is the mystery of how we, after undergoing some kind of death, receive new life and new spirit."

Jesus himself showed forth the pattern of this paschal mystery in his death and resurrection. In this paschal cycle Rolheiser points out five clear, distinct moments:

- Good Friday: the loss of life—the disciples were *dispirited*, as the spirit had been knocked out of them
- Easter Sunday: the emergence of Jesus in his resurrected life

- The forty days in which Jesus appeared and taught his disciples his last things, giving them time to adjust to the fact that he would be leaving them
- Ascension: when he taught them not to cling to him but to let the "old days" go
- Pentecost: when they received the gift of the Spirit for the next stage, living out the mission that Jesus had begun

Each of these "moments" is an essential part of the transformation into new life, yet too often we skip over one of the most important among them: the "forty days" of grieving the old and being prepared to receive the new. This is an absolutely crucial time that we must not pass over or rush through.

"Life goes on. It's time to move on." I remember people saying this to us in a time of loss. Their words were well-meant but cruel and very unhelpful when we were caught in the depths of darkness and grief.

Indeed life does go on, and should go on, and God will give us what we need for each challenge we face. But as the disciples waited forty days between Jesus' death and resurrection and the coming of the Spirit at Pentecost, we must allow our spirit time — time to grieve the old, to be prepared to let go and receive the gift of the Spirit that we need for our new life. So the paschal mystery calls us to enter fully into the darkness but then to move into ascension and Pentecost.

A woman who was abused as a child, and had been crippled by the memory of that abuse for forty years, felt that the spirit had gone out of her. What helped her was to be reminded that "Jesus gave the disciples forty days to grieve and adjust. He has given you forty years! It is time to let go."

Recasting the paschal mystery into terms that are personal for each of us, Rolheiser puts it like this.

1. Name your deaths.
2. Claim your births.
3. Grieve what you have lost and adjust to the new reality.
4. Do not cling to the old, let it ascend and give you its blessing.
5. Accept the spirit of the life that you are in fact living.

Over the stairway in our daughter's house is a painting, *I Reach for You,* that seems to beautifully symbolize this paschal cycle. A woman stands at the bottom of a dark green hill. Her arms are lifted toward a lavender sky. A bright yellow balloon she has released soars up. This scene spoke so powerfully to Debbie and Craig when their oldest son, Graham, was leaving for college that they bought it. It seemed to Debbie as if she were the one lifting her arms to let him go and opening her heart to what might come next. The poignant transition is captured not so much in the dark trees of the hill as in the vivid colors of balloon and sky that reach out to enfold her as she lifts her arms toward them. It is a picture of light shining into the folds of a heart. She is letting the old ascend, to give her its blessing.

WHAT HAVE BEEN YOUR DARKNESSES?

I do not enjoy the dark times. I would never choose them. Yet I know that those are precisely the times when I have grown deeper, have been stretched to become stronger, and ultimately have known most clearly what it means to be unconditionally loved, beyond all reason and expectation.

"What were your own darknesses," a friend wrote to me, "and what did God reveal about himself in each of these? What gifts did he give?" I pondered and wrote back that for me they included the following:

- the darkness of doubt and absence—bringing the gift of being deeply loved

- the darkness of depression — the gift of being valued for who I am
- the darkness of denial — the gift of a deeper honesty
- the darkness of deep disappointment — the gifts of new sons and daughters
- the darkness of disconnection, of aging — the gift to live more fully now
- the darkness of betrayal and attack — the gift of knowing that integrity does not mean to live in perfection but in the truth of who I am

I could elaborate on my darknesses. Instead let me suggest that you put down the book and make your own list, naming, if you can, the gifts you have received, the light that has reached you through those darknesses.

Light carries two meanings: it can be the opposite of darkness and also the opposite of heaviness. Through the paschal mystery God can transform both darkness into light and burden into blessing. Helen Luke illumines this second meaning in her wise reflections on aging and suffering. Words about suffering have a heavy, foreboding ring. To be afflicted is to be struck down. To be depressed is to be pressed down. Yet if we learn to embrace suffering, to carry it rather than lying under its weight and letting ourselves be crushed, then something strange happens: "We have lifted the weight and instead of being crushed by it we find it extraordinarily light — 'My yoke is easy, my burden is light.' The pain remains but it is more like the piercing of a sword than a weight."

THE VIEW FROM HURRICANE RIDGE:
LOVE IN THE DEEPEST PLACES

There was no hurricane on Hurricane Ridge as I stood there one early August morning, high in the Olympic mountain range above Port Angelus, Washington, looking out at one of the most dazzling stretches of landscape I had ever seen. It looked as if morning had broken over the whole world in one shining moment.

To the south I looked up at the glistening glacial peaks of the Olympic range, with Mount Olympus towering above them all. Northward I could see across the straits of Juan de Fuca to Victoria, Canada, from forty miles away a mere smudge on the morning horizon.

The breadth of it! A fellow hiker passing by remarked, "I have never been any place where you could see so far and wide in every direction—with nothing to block the view." I agreed. Wherever I looked the panorama seemed to be without limits.

Plunging below were incisions where glaciers had once cut deep valleys; they gave a sense of both invitation and danger. On one steep ridge I heard an alarmed older woman call out to her adult son as he knelt to take a photo: "Come back. Please come back! You are too close to the edge. You are scaring me!"

It was almost impossible to take in the magnificent creation of God, spreading as far as I could see in every direction.

I was making my way home from my usual summer study retreat in Vancouver. This year it had been just a bit disappointing, as the condo I usually stay in, with a magnificent view over English Bay, had not been available due to illness in the owner's family. Further, an eagerly awaited visit with some friends had not worked out. I had left Vancouver a bit early and had a free day to spend before catching my plane home from Seattle.

On the spur of the moment I had taken a ferry to Victoria and then squeezed into the very last space on another ferry to Port Angelus. I called my son-in-law Craig, who had been there the year before, and he gave me the name of a B&B to stay in. He had also suggested I go to Hurricane Ridge. "One of the most spectacular views I have ever seen," he told me.

Arriving in Port Angelus in late afternoon, I grabbed a Subway sandwich and took the seventeen-mile drive to Hurricane Ridge to see the sunset from the top. Two miles from the top, a beep told me I was running low on gas. Not relishing the thought of having to coast down on an empty tank, I turned back. That night I went to bed nursing my small disappointments.

But the next morning when I reached the top, all the let-down feelings blew away like mountain breezes that wipe away morning mist.

My mind went back to a morning a few days before, when I sat with my Bible in my lap and gazed at Vancouver's English Bay, hemmed by distant hills. I had just read Paul's eloquent prayer asking that his fellow believers might be able "to comprehend, with all the saints, what is the breadth and length and height and depth, and to know the love of Christ that surpasses knowledge" (Eph 3:18-19).

I wondered whether when Paul wrote those words he perhaps was picturing the high peaks of the Taurus mountain range thirty miles from his home in Tarsus, which he had climbed as a boy, and the wide view of the Mediterranean shore, just ten miles away.

As I drank in the view from Hurricane Ridge, the thought came: *If this magnificent creation is almost overwhelming in its scope, how much more the love of God!* The words of an old song came back to me:

> Higher than the highest mountain,
> deeper than the deepest sea,
> wider than the widest ocean
> is my Savior's love for me.

A MAN IN THE VALLEY

Not long after my Hurricane Ridge epiphany I had lunch with a man who was going through the deepest, darkest valley of his life. Such valley journeys come to all of us at various places and times.

This valley was one he had entered as the consequence of his own indiscreet actions.

What could I say to him to be of any help? Certainly not clichés, well wishes or just good advice. But I could share some of my own valley times and the knowledge that my deepest sense of being loved has also grown out of the depths.

I also told him of my thoughts as two weeks before I stood on Hurricane Ridge. As I admitted to my friend, I would much prefer to experience God's love in the high and wide and long places rather than in the depths! To remember the high and bracing places, the peak experiences of life, is gratifying. To recall how God has been with me no matter how far flung my life has been, as I have moved and lived or traveled in more than forty countries: that is fulfilling. To be able to look back over the vista of more than seventy years of life, from boyhood in a small Canadian city to the morning I scanned the glorious vista in the Pacific Northwest: that is cause for gratitude.

But why would I want to pass through the long, dark, deep and lonesome valleys—even if God says he will be with me there?

Again I think of the view from Hurricane Ridge, the contrast of the high, glittering mountains towering over the valleys. The entire effect was magnificent. Without the cut and contrast of the valleys, the incisions made across the years by glacial masses and the unending tumbling of waters on the rocks, like the furrows plowed by the weight of years on the face of an old man or woman—without the depths the heights would not exist or appear so magnificent.

I spoke to my friend of Corrie ten Boom, whose own face bore the signs of her suffering in Hitler's concentration camps for her attempts to hide Jews from the Nazi troops in her native Holland. Corrie used to say, "There is no pit so deep that his love is not deeper still."

As I related my story and her words, my friend nodded; tears came to his eyes as he told me how in the midst of his own current crushing time, his father, for the first time in thirty years, had said to him, "Son, I love you."

THE DIMENSIONS OF LOVE

Those words I read in Vancouver (and recalled on Hurricane Ridge) about the dimensions of God's love—the height and length and width and the depth of it—led me to do a little exercise to reflect on my own life.

How long . . .

I drew a chart, dividing my life into eight chronological segments, to recall *how long* God's love had been in terms of the trajectory of my life and travels.

How wide . . .

Then I superimposed on the chart a series of maplike drawings showing the unfolding of the "wheres" of my life's journey, spreading from boyhood in Canada to a worldwide ministry and now folding back to a more limited circle nearer to home.

How high and how deep . . .

On another page I drew a chart showing the major emotional and spiritual highs and lows across the years. Where were my peaks? Where were the valleys? And where had God been in all of this?

In my journal I wrote, "How long—the roads traveled, the trajectories and flight patterns. So long has been the companionship, the guidance of my Divine Lord and Loving Friend." I also copied down words of Ronald Rolheiser: faith is "to see everything against an infinite horizon," and "there is in the lives of every one of us a conspiracy of accidents, that might aptly be called divine providence."

As I wrote, sitting by English Bay in Vancouver, looking at the long horizon and the hills in the distance, I thought of how much lay beyond and how much lay behind me. As grateful as I am for the mountaintop times, perhaps I am even more so for the divine "accidents" that came at the low points and valleys of my life—the hands of my wife on my face during a dark time of depression, helping me to know I was truly loved . . . the men who met with me weekly after our son died . . . the young leaders who showed me their love and trust at a time when I felt very unjustly accused and attacked by people projecting their own darkness onto me.

OUT OF THE DEPTHS

These were little signs of grace in dark nights, the signs that the psalmist (was it David?) must have been looking for when he wrote Psalm 130.

"Out of the depths I cry to you, O LORD," he began, words that Anton Boisen chose as the title of his classic book on depression. Whatever experience of the psalmist lay behind these words, the cry was one of desperate urgency: "Hear my voice! Let your ears be attentive to the voice of my supplications." He is bold: *hear me!* No politeness here, just sheer need.

It is also the cry of one who stands stripped naked by life, acknowledging both his own sin and his only hope. "If you, O LORD, should mark iniquities, Lord, who could stand? But there is forgiveness with you, so that you may be revered."

Then, after the desperation and the humbling a quietness descends, as if with a sigh of his heart he lets go of any demand and simply affirms:

I wait for the LORD, my souls waits,

and in his word I hope:
my soul waits for the LORD
   more than those who watch for the morning
   more than those who watch for the morning.

That quiet repetition will strike a chord in anyone who has known what it is to lie sleepless, in pain of body or soul or mind, waiting, waiting for the long night to pass, hoping for morning finally to come so the soul can sing with fresh confidence as the psalmist does:

O Israel, hope in the LORD!
For with the LORD there is steadfast love,
   and with him is great power to redeem.
It is he who will redeem Israel
   from all its iniquities.

And not only Israel, but us too who wait for light in the dark places.

My friend who came to talk with me had dug a deep hole, deep enough that he wondered whether he could dig his way out. He wept as he realized how he had disappointed so many by his actions. He wondered whether and when morning would come to him. At the same time he was mourning the disappointments that he himself had endured, the unfulfilled longings in his relationships. There was no sense of blaming others, just a resigned sadness at what had never been and now might never be.

As I listened to him, my mind went back to the small disappointments I had that summer, when arrangements for a place to stay and a meeting with good friends fell through due to unavoidable circumstances, and then to a passage that spoke to me about the inevitable disappointments that come because of the finite nature of human love: "The first task in any love, whether in a marriage or in a deep friendship, is for the two persons to console each other for the limits of their love, for the fact that they cannot not disappoint each other."

Our love is always limited, inadequate and wounded. Emotionally and spiritually we are like Grand Canyons with a floor beneath our reach. We search and search to find the "perfect" friend or lover or mate who can meet all our needs. But only when we give up on our messianic expectations can we be set free truly to love, in a reflection of God's highest and widest, longest and deepest love for us.

The psalmist learned this secret as, surrendering his demands, he could begin to say, "I wait for the LORD. My soul waits, and in his word I hope."

Carlo Carletto, who had spent many years in the desert alone with God, was asked what he had heard from God. His simple reply: "God is telling us: learn to wait—wait—wait for your God, wait for love."

FINDING HURRICANE RIDGE AGAIN
When I started to write this chapter, we had just learned that our daughter Debbie had cancer. Again. Seven years ago she had a mastectomy, and each year since tests indicated she was cancer free. Now another malignancy had occurred in the same location. Once again we were entering a long, dark, narrow valley.

I wished I could make the seventeen-mile drive up the mountain road, stand on Hurricane Ridge, feel the morning sun burning away the heaviness from my mind, the fresh breeze blowing the anxiety from my soul, could lift my eyes to the far hills above and the rolling sea in the distance and the vast sweep to the long horizon, see the deep valleys below as part of a larger whole.

But Hurricane Ridge was a continent away. For the challenge of this day, or any day, I need other paths, leading to nearer ridges for my soul, places that breathe fresh hope.

Prayer is the quickest path, of course. My first words to God about Debbie were a cry of protest: "No, God. Not again. We lost one child years ago. We can't lose another one." It was protest, but it was also honest prayer. Later we would calm down a bit, hug each other, hear encouraging words from the skillful surgeon who would operate, successfully, again on her.

So that morning my prayer was also one of lifting up. As I took my usual walk, I prayed the same morning prayer I have used for years: "To you, O LORD, I lift up my soul; in you I trust, O my God. . . . Show me your ways, O LORD, teach me your paths; guide me in your truth and teach me, for you are God my Savior, and my hope is in you all day long" (Ps 25:1-5 NIV).

Scripture makes a way, especially those parts that I have lived with during and after hard times. Psalm 130, quoted above, takes on fresh meaning for me:

> Out of the depths I cry to you, O LORD . . .
> I wait for the LORD, my soul waits
>   and in his word I hope . . .
>   more than those who wait for the morning.

I also repeat to myself parts of Psalm 116, a psalm of thanksgiving which I had learned by heart and repeated daily with gratitude during recovery from a heart attack:

> I love the LORD, for he heard my voice;
>   he heard my cry for mercy . . .
>   when I was in great need, he saved me.
> Be at rest once more, O my soul,
>   for the LORD has been good to you. (vv. 1, 6-7 NIV)

Those Scriptures are old friends that I have lived with and walked with. Their very familiarity comforts me, enlarges my vision, reminds me how God has been with us through hard times. They are a present help! Would they be so if I had not learned and lived with them before crisis broke uninvited into our lives? Now they take me, so to speak, by the hand and the heart and lead me up the ridge.

So do friends who have been companions on the way. Jeanie and I were helped by calls from John and Anne, a couple we walked with when they lost a beloved daughter some years ago. Now they share our tears, understand our fears, give us words of practical encouragement. Another time when I was in a tight place John called and said, "Leighton, you are so close to the situation right now you can't see beyond it. Take a step back from the table in your mind, breathe deep and try to take a wider view." It wasn't easy—but I tried, and it helped.

Books on our shelves are also guides up the trail, especially the ones by wise travelers on the upward (or downward!) way in years past. I remember reading to Jeanie words from the Scottish preacher Alexander Whyte. Commenting on the very prayer of Paul's that I read by English Bay about the love of Christ that passes (and surpasses) knowledge, he writes:

> The love of Christ has no border: it has no shore: it has no bottom. The love of Christ is boundless: it is bottomless: it is infinite: it is divine. That it passeth knowledge is the greatest thing that ever was said, or could be said, about it. . . . We shall come to the shore, we shall strike the bottom of every other love: but never of the love of Christ! . . . You, who have once cast yourself into it, and upon it—the great mystic speaks of it as if it were at once an ocean and a mountain,— you will never come to the length of it, or to the breadth of it, or to the depth of it, or to the height of it. To all eternity, the love of Christ to you will be new.

OTHER WAYS TO HURRICANE RIDGE

There are also special places that open the soul to fresh hope. "Thin places" the old Celts used to call them, places where the veil between earth and heaven seems nearly transparent, such as where land and water meet. For me, one such place is an hour north of where we live, the lakeside home of friends who leave a key hanging outside so I can use it whenever I wish for a quiet day.

On a mid-September day I headed there in early morning. As I stopped for breakfast, a kind of "Hurricane Ridge moment" came in a heart-moving and new (to me) setting of John Rutter's "Pie Jesu" played on my favorite classical music station.

It came also in the eastern sky. Stepping out of the car, I saw shafts of light breaking through the clouds. One central, shining, large-winged shape stretched out to each side like a dove, or an angel. At the very top it appeared like a robed and luminous figure with hands outstretched—as if the risen Jesus himself might be greeting me at the break of day.

It came in an e-mail from a friend, who told me that she had to sort out in prayer an ongoing resentment and realized the root was the fear of being hurt again. "The same thing is true for you right now in regard to this news. You are afraid of getting hurt again through another horrific loss." She quoted Philippians 4:6-7, which had helped her to focus, and ended:

> Behind that anxiousness is our human finiteness wrapped in fear. Instead of fear, God invites us to name it before him, with a heart of eternal gratitude for the eternal wholeness we have in him. . . . I am praying that you will see God watching over your heart and mind as a mother hen watches over her chicks. Blessings on your valley, friend.

A way to "Hurricane Ridge" came also from Scripture. When I got to the lake, I sat by the water and read over and over those words of Paul: "Do not worry about anything, but in everything by prayer and supplication with thanksgiving let your requests be made known to God. And the peace of God, which surpasses all understanding, will guard your hearts and your minds in Christ Jesus (Phil 4:6-7).

In my journal I wrote "Why so anxious? Fear of what?" and listed everything I could think of that was a cause for anxiety and fear. There were thirteen items (and more I added later!), from the fear of another horrific loss like that of our son Sandy in 1981 to the worry that Deb's cancer might have spread.

Then, taking the lead from Paul, next to each anxiety I wrote a reason for thanks—and a matching request. Next to my fear of another loss I wrote a thanksgiving—"for someone to love so much" (as we did Sandy, and do Deb and our son Kevin)—and a request: "Don't let Deb die."

At the end of the morning I wrote that just as high on Hurricane Ridge I had been captivated by "the love of Christ that surpasses knowledge," so here by the lake "I ask for the peace of God that surpasses understanding."

Later that day I headed home, back to the valley that stretched out for weeks ahead. But I went with a new confidence, a fresh trust. God had provided a sacred place, the words of friends, signs in the clouds, strong advice from Scripture, the opening up of my own heart to create another high place, a ridge of the soul, from which I could find a way through the deeps of the days ahead.

Practicing Attentiveness: Guard of the Heart

Thomas Keating recommends a practice he calls *guard of the heart* as a way to note and release the emotions that weigh us down. When some particular "darkness"—grief, anger, doubt—weighs in, he suggests three ways to deal with it. One is to turn back to whatever we are doing. Another is to turn our attention to some other occupation. The third and most important is to turn that feeling over to Christ. I have tried to follow his advice by asking myself, for example: What prompted these tears, or this anger, or hurt, or desire? What do they connect to in me? Often I can identify a need for love, for security, for understanding. I pause just long enough to recall that God alone can fully meet that need or longing. Then as best I can I give those thoughts over to God — almost as the woman in Debbie's painting lets go of the balloon — and move on. So I pay attention to the feelings. Accept them. Let them go. And turn my attention to what comes next.

One Who Paid Attention
Jerry Sittser Trying to Catch the Sun

CAN YOU IMAGINE WHAT IT WOULD BE LIKE to lose three generations of your closest family in one blinding moment? How would you survive? That happened in 1991 to Jerry Sittser, a professor at Whitworth University in Spokane, Washington.

He, his wife Lynda, their four children and his mother Grace, had been to a Native American powwow in Idaho. As they were returning home late, a car with a drunk driver going eighty-five miles an hour swerved out and crashed into them head-on. In an instant Sittser lost his mother, his wife and their youngest daughter.

In *A Grace Disguised* Sittser describes with searing honesty what it was like to be a single father, a teacher, a counselor to others while he himself was a man bereft and torn, slipping into a black hole of oblivion and often simply wanting out.

One night he had a kind of "waking dream." The sun was setting, and he was frantically chasing after it toward the west, hoping to catch it and bring it back. But it was a losing race. Soon the sun was gone, and he "felt a vast darkness closing in."

Shortly after this, his sister Diane told him that the quickest way to reach the sun is not to go west but instead to head east, to move fully "into the darkness until one comes to the sunrise."

It was a counterintuitive insight that helped Sittser find a road to recovery: "I discovered in that moment that I had the power to choose the direction my life would head. . . . I decided from that point on to walk into the darkness rather than try to outrun it, to let my experience of loss take me on a journey wherever it would lead, and to allow myself to be transformed by my suffering rather than to think I could somehow avoid it."

8   Lighting the Lamps

The House with Golden Windows

Then you, God, are the guest whom
he receives in gentle evening hours.
RAINER MARIA RILKE,
PARAPHRASED BY DAVID STEINDL-RAST

Be at rest once more, O my soul,
* for the LORD has been good to you.*
PSALM 116:7 NIV

In the course of the daily hours, Vespers celebrates the lighting of the lamps as evening descends. It is a counterpart to Lauds, with its salute to the morning light. In the words of David Steindl-Rast,

> Vespers is the hour that invites peace of heart, which is the reconciling of the contradictions within ourselves and around us. . . . Within this evening hour, when we become festive in a new way and receive God as a guest, we stretch that compass of time beyond time and embrace the now. That's the serenity, the peace of heart, the ability to embrace the inevitable contradictions the day leaves behind, which is the mood of Vespers.

> Sometimes, after the sun has set, the clouds begin to glow with colors of water and colors of fire. Buildings and mountains also glow, and the sun is reflected like molten gold in the windows of far-away houses.

MOON SHINE STILL
Domain Park, Sydney, 2005

I walked one more time, later afternoon
from the busy boulevard across the fields
where boys play rugby on the grassy top
over the parking decks for the Domain
past the smaller park by St. Mary's Cathedral
where the trees are dying now, poisoned by the ground.
Paradise lost, by a parking lot.

Through the screen of a spreading tree I saw
poised above Sydney harbor
a waxing early evening moon, coming on
as slowly as a fluorescent lamp
its face nearly full
with makeup in pale blue
waiting patiently in the wings of evening
for its turn.

Below, the blaze of brother sun
almost finished with his daily run
his rays setting fire to the buildings up on King's Cross
making their very drabness glow
with a kind of glory
like latter-day saints.

I sat then for a long time on a remote bench
above the darkening bay,
next to a wide and winding old gum tree,
watching the ferries end their day
as they made their dim and final crossings
to and from Manley,
recollecting the crossings of my life,
my own waxings and wanings
at just the time when evening blue bids good night
to youthful days.

Walking back I went slowly now,
careful with my footsteps in the dusk
trying not to stumble on a root
past the old sick trees
marked for mercy killing.

When I scanned the sky again
the moon was almost fully waxed
shining out more clearly
with a brighter, bluer face against the dark
in the lateness of the day

May my moonshine
(I breathed)
may my moonshine
shine more brightly still
and make me thankful for these later days.

SYDNEY, SEPTEMBER 15, 2005

There is something almost magical to me about that border time between afternoon and evening when the sun is setting and casting its glow. Sunset (the "vespers hour), like sunrise, is a liminal, in-between time. Like the rest in a musical score, it calls us to pause, to come to a stop between light and night, busyness and quietness, between winding up and winding down.

Late afternoon takes my mind back a long time, to the years when our Debbie was little and every night that I was home I told her a bedtime story. Almost invariably she would insist, "Daddy, tell me about the house with golden windows."

Whether it was a story I made up or one I had read I do not remember, but it was about a father and his little daughter walking at the end of day and in the distance seeing a house "with golden windows."

Entranced, they walk quickly toward that house, but as they draw nearer the golden windows disappear and the windows become just plain old glass. They walk away, and then just as suddenly the golden windows reappear.

At last the little girl exclaims with sudden recognition, "Daddy, that's our house! But why does it only *seem* to have golden windows?"

The father replies, "Every house has golden windows if you only look closely and carefully enough, at the right time."

With a sigh of wonder and contentment, Debbie would slip off into sleep.

The lure of those golden windows speaks to the universal longing for home in almost every human heart, a longing that often seems to summon us with a special pathos at Vespers.

THE IN-BETWEEN TIMES

What are the afternoon times of our lives? They could be almost any "in-between" time: after work and before shutting down for the night; between jobs or assignments; perhaps the time of engagement or pregnancy. Afternoons can be down times of rest after a very busy period—perhaps a sabbatical. In the seasons of our life, afternoons are the autumn, the season of midlife when the curve of our energy begins to drop.

Afternoon is also a time to rest and enjoy the fullness of what life has to offer, as well as to let go of regrets over what may have passed us by. Yet it is a time not of retreat but of renewal, a time to explore and develop new and overlooked parts of ourselves.

Late afternoon and early evening are often special times in the stories of the Bible. In "the cool of the evening" God walked with Adam and Eve in the quietness of Eden. Johann Sebastian Bach chooses an evening setting in his *St. Matthew Passion*, reminding us that it was in the evening, when the floodwaters had diminished, that Noah's dove returned to the ark bringing back in its beak an olive branch. It was evening also when Jesus was laid to rest. On a later evening Jesus accepted the invitation to dine with the two discouraged disciples he met on the road to Emmaus, and over that supper they recognized him "in the breaking of the bread."

This is most especially the time to make fresh room for God in our heart. Rainer Maria Rilke put this beautifully into the image of weaving together the strands of our life:

> She who reconciles the ill-matched threads
> of her life, and weaves them gratefully
> into a single cloth—
> it's she who drives the loudmouths from the hall
> and clears it for a different celebration,
>
> where the one guest is you.
> In the softness of evening
> it's you she receives.

Or as another translates his words:

> Then you, God, are the guest
> whom he receives in gentle evening hours

THERE IS A RIVER

Late-afternoon thoughts often take me back to a small town in Scotland with the magical name of Dunkeld, on the road that runs north from Perth to the Highlands.

In the summer of 1955 I had just been ordained. Jeanie and I were setting out on a lifetime of ministry and had gone to Scotland for a summer-long preaching tour. With two musician friends we were headed for meetings along the north coast.

Looking for a place to spend the night, we had spotted a sign pointing to Dunkeld House. When we turned off, we were rewarded with one of the most charming evenings of our young lives. Down a long lane we came to a private home that had been made into a small country hotel.

It was a dream of a place. The gardens, the old stone house, the manicured croquet lawn, the quiet dining room and delicious food, the setting by the flowing River Tay all made for a long, clear and unforgettable summer evening.

So when fifty years later we planned a trip to Scotland, we decided to see if Dunkeld House still was there. An Internet search confirmed a hotel with that name, and we made reservations for a night.

Could it be the same place? As we turned down the long, narrow country lane, we knew it was. There in the calm light of late afternoon were the green hills and the tiny lambs playing by the side of their mothers. To our left, beyond a white fence, were ruins of an ancient cathedral church, through the trees was a glimpse of the River Tay, and finally we came to a white-stucco building trimmed in red.

It had certainly changed, with a large, modern reception area and a bar and restaurant much more elegant than we remembered. It was now an upscale resort, with a convention of trucking executives arriving.

When we stepped outside onto the patio in full view of the river, rimmed by century-old trees, we reconnected with the Dunkeld of our memories.

Later, as Jeanie took a nap, I wandered out to the river. Suddenly a shower of rain, lit up by the late afternoon sun, came spattering into the river—so vivid that I could almost count individual raindrops.

Along the bank, following the flow downstream, I watched the

river go under a bridge and bend away. Where does it go, I wondered, and where has it come from? Where are the years that have
flowed since we first stopped here?

After dinner I read from an old book by Scottish preacher Alexander Whyte. Frayed at the edges, it was given to me by Jeanie's
mother, Morrow Coffey Graham. I came across a passage marked
with a red pen about a "fast-ageing saint" who at the end of each
day prayed:

> I give Thee thanks, O Lord. Evening draws nigh: make it
> bright. For as day has its evening, so has life. The evening of life
> is old age, and old age is fast overtaking me: make it bright. . . .
> Let the fast-coming close of my life be believing, acceptable,
> sinless, fearless: and, if it please thee, painless. And let me out-
> strip the night, doing, with all my might, some good work.

When Mother Graham marked those words she was in her late
fifties, already suffering from osteoporosis and feeling the aging of
her body. But she still had "some good work" to do, including several hundred letters she handwrote in her eighty-sixth year to various students and missionaries.

As I read my throat tightened. In the dusk by the river I found
myself in tears. Why? For the passage of time? For our youthful
selves recalled and gone? For a longtime friend and spiritual father
whose memorial service I had just attended? Yes. For all those
memories.

But also for more. For that sense of longing that, like the River
Tay running beside me, flowed through my heart. A longing not so
much to walk again along the river of memories as to know where
the river yet leads. A longing for what is still ahead, as ancient as
these green hills and the river that flows through them. A longing
that in the quietest of moments springs up again and again in the
human heart.

PEACE LIKE A RIVER

On that same Scotland journey I brought along for bedtime reading Leif Enger's captivating novel *Peace like a River.* Set in a Minnesota small town in the 1960s, the story is narrated by ten-year-
old Reuben. His older brother, Davy, has broken out of jail after
being convicted for deliberately shooting down two young ruffians
who broke into the family's house one night.

Davy and Reuben's father, Jeremiah, a single parent who sup-
ports his three children by working as a school janitor, has a strong
intuition that his son has fled west. After much prayer he is convinced that they must go after him. In one twenty-four-hour period
he is fired from his job, sells some of their possessions, packs up the
rest, shutters their house, and with Reuben and daughter Swede (a
precocious child who write ballads about the Old West) heads for
the Dakotas in a trailer inherited from a friend. Like the shepherd
seeking the lost sheep and the sweeping woman a lost coin in
Jesus' stories, they set out to find their lost son and brother.

Along their way, Davy's seeking family is helped by various
characters, tricked by others, and tracked by a government agent
who is sure they will lead him to Davy.

In the badlands of western North Dakota they meet Roxanne, a
goodhearted woman who sells them gas on a Sunday and gives
them a room for the night. When a huge snowstorm strands them,
her house becomes a way-station on their journey. From her backyard, Reuben spots Davy on horseback on a far ridge. Davy gives
in to Reuben's pleas to show him his hiding place, and there Reuben meets a fierce and dangerous mountain man hiding from the
law who for devious reasons has given Davy shelter.

As the story comes to a dramatic crisis, Davy is encircled by the
forces closing in on him: the FBI agent narrowing his search, the
treacherous mountain man, his own seeking family. It is as if (al-

most in an acted-out version of the classic theology of the book of Romans) he is hounded by the trinity of law, evil and grace.

In the denouement, law loses out. The government man is ambushed and killed by the sinister outlaw. And grace leads to a homecoming. The family turns back to Minnesota, joined by Roxanne.

But evil has not finished. The mountain man who couldn't root the goodness out of Davy follows them home and with a sniper rifle tries to shoot Davy. He misses but takes down both father Jeremiah and Reuben.

If that had been all, there would be no "peace like a river." But then Reuben, on his sickbed, has a vision. He comes to a wide river, across which there is a place where "no sun shines in the sky, so days do not pass . . . the light seems a work of the air itself . . . a country more real than ours. . . . Its stone is harder, its water more drenching . . . a city where the longer you looked, the more you saw."

Somehow he crosses the river and somehow is unsurprised at having done so. He laughs in place of language as he feels prodded on "to appear before the master. The place had a master!"

Ahead of him, along another river, runs a man: his father. Together they become part of a huge throng of people moving like a great river toward a city with turrets.

Reuben thinks, "Lord, can't I be among them? Can't I come in too?"

"*Soon,*" says Jeremiah. He takes his son's hand: "Take care of Davy." His father is going on. Reuben is going back. For both of them the "stream was singing aloud."

Peace, at the end, flowed like a river.

When I read this final episode, my throat tightened and my eyes blurred. The tears were not just from this story but from the day many years before when our son Sandy died during heart surgery, and the imaginary conversations I had with him afterward about heaven, and how he could "think so deeply and every thought was clear . . . run and never get tired . . . so surefooted in the paths of glory."

More than anytime in the years since, when I read Reuben's description of heaven, I could pray: "God, thank you that if Sandy cannot be here, he is there."

The story of this family's journey to seek Davy touched my soul deeply, resonating with the human longing for completeness, to reconnect with the missing parts of ourselves and those to whom we "long to belong."

Yet even with the vision of heaven, the river does not flow with perfect peace in this world. The novel ends in incompleteness. Davy is not restored to his family and community. Instead he finds refuge in a small Canadian town, where once in a long while Reuben visits him.

The city with turrets, with a river running through it, real as it is, is still a city we see from a distance, a better country that we long for and look forward to. The river is "already" and "not yet."

And is this not precisely how we wake up in the world? As Ronald Rolheiser writes regarding "holy longing": "Sensing that we are incomplete . . . cut off, a little piece of something was once was part of a whole . . . we experience ourselves as white or yolk, separated from our other half."

It is a holy longing because the desire that fuels our restlessness is at its core a longing for the God who made us for himself.

Perhaps that is why in the gloaming of a Scottish evening, with rain showers falling amid sunshine, I could stand by the River Tay, remember the lovely evening so many years before, know how much I loved my wife sleeping in our room, and still find myself with tears of longing for what had been and what must yet be.

Is that not where the roots of our restlessness lie?

Jeanie thinks I have "restless legs syndrome." A good portion of my 6'4" height comes from the knees down the shins to the ground, and whether or not that is the reason for the syndrome, I am a restless sleeper.

Restlessness makes an appearance in my vocational life as well. Those of us who are called to lead are not easily satisfied or willing to take things for granted. I have found myself always probing, reading, listening, pushing the frontiers. But there is a downside to always reaching farther. "You don't have to be the best at absolutely everything," Jeanie sometimes reminds me with an affectionate (and exasperated) shake of her head.

French philosopher and mathematician Blaise Pascal observed that most of our human problems come because we don't know how to sit still in our room for an hour. Restless legs are one thing; a restless heart is quite another.

THE FLOW OF MY SOUL

As I sat in solitude by the River Tay in Scotland that late spring evening, I remembered that the ancient philosopher Heraclitus said it was impossible to step into the same river twice, for a river is always in flux. The flow of the river for fifty years and centuries before was a reminder of the restless moving on that has marked my life, the travels in more than forty countries of the world, the changes of ministry focus, the friends made and lost and passed on, the homes we have lived in.

Yet Heraclitus left out an important truth. A river is more than a succession of millions of disparate drops of water. I can step into a river in this living moment and know it has *never* changed. For each moment of time, each part of creation, each aspect of my life is also lived under the eye of God and is gathered and held in his eternal hand.

So as I watched the flow of the Tay I murmured words that had been playing over and over in my mind for weeks from Psalm 116:7 (NIV):

Be at rest once more, O my soul,
for the LORD has been good to you.

The 116th Psalm is one of thanksgiving for healing, so the psalmist's words brought to mind other words that my son-in-law Craig had given me after a heart attack arrested me:

In returning and rest you shall be saved;
in quietness and in trust shall be your strength. (Is 30:15)

For months I prayed these words each time I took a morning walk, and I wrote them out in my journal daily. They became a reminder to slow down, to savor the goodness of the Lord each moment, to remind myself that I did not have to "do it now" every time a new thought came, to ruthlessly eliminate hurry from my life and soul.

But we human beings easily forget and slip back into old patterns of mindless activity. So as I returned to the admonition to "be at rest once more . . ." I did a little soul check-up. In my journal I wrote,

My soul is restless—so often moving out, reaching, pursuing, whether romantic dreams or impressive performances—or another "home." Every once in a while something else is my fancy. Come home, soul!

A year ago it was time to rest—heart attack now down-stream. I felt fully recovered yet more conscious of my vulnerable body—not aging so much as more fragile. My soul is a strange mix of gratitude and restlessness. I want—need—to be at rest in the goodness of God.

As I watched the stream go by and as the psalm went through

my mind on the banks of the Tay, I realized that to return to Scotland was also to appreciate what a rich and poignant tapestry life has been, full of joy and sadness, a reprise of what has been and will not be, and will yet be.

The rest I long for is not static, like the rest of death. It is "peace like a river," constant yet always moving on, sometimes fast and turbulent like the whitewater I have rafted on in the North Carolina mountains, at other times quieter like the slow eddies of the Tay, but always the peace of "living waters" which Jesus promised would flow out of the very center of those who stayed close to him.

Why then is my soul so often restless? Why do I try so hard to fill any empty spaces? Why do I find it hard to sit for an hour and simply *be* and remember God's goodness?

Why, as the poet May Sarton writes, have I so much of my life

Run madly, as if Time were there,
Terribly old, crying a warning,
"Hurry, you will be dead before —"
(What? Before you reach the morning?
Or the end of the poem is clear?
Or love safe in the walled city?)

In part it is simply the way I am made. But more than from restless legs, it comes from a restless soul — the human condition, the "God-shaped vacuum" of Pascal's famous metaphor.

Like Davy and his family in Leif Enger's novel, we live between exile and homecoming. There is, the story seems to say, no perfect ending yet, not until we finally come to the River of Paradise. Even when we have come to the Father through Jesus and found our true place, we still live between the "already" and the "not yet." As Paul writes in Romans, the Spirit affirms that we are indeed God's children, yet the Spirit also groans within while we are in the midst of the birth pangs of the new creation.

So our rest and our restlessness—the search for wholeness and the longing for home—will always have these two parts to it, the sense of being at home already and the longing for "a better country, that is, a heavenly one" (Heb 11:16).

Thomas Keating maintains that we spend the first part of our lives finding our role—what we are conditioned by our culture to *do*—and the next part finding our true selves, what we are called by God to *be*. He teaches that through a spiritual practice like centering prayer, in which we learn to let go of our clamoring, insistent everyday thoughts and drives and to rest simply in the presence of God, we experience a divine therapy and deep rest.

For me those moments by the river were a kind of centering prayer, letting thoughts go like the leaves floating down the surface of the river while the spirit sinks into the depths. A time to reflect on the question, what is true rest?

KNOWING HOW TO STOP

I know how to be busy and to move purposefully. Do I also know how to stop?

In music, a *rest* is a pause, a space not filled. *Arrest* (coming from the French *arreter* meaning to stop) is a halting of the normal flow of events. So a criminal is *arrested* from his nefarious deeds, or my brother-in-law's heart goes into *arrest* (as it did last year). Something *arresting* makes us stop and pay attention.

What was it then about the stop at Dunkeld that made it true rest? It was an arresting moment, a confluence of the River Tay and the river of memory. The very flowing of the river was a reminder of what has outlasted the years.

The "beauty of repose" was in that place—the river so graceful, the trees bending over, the shower in the sunlight, the structures old and new in the building.

The quiet of thought, the reflection in the mirror of my mind of the prayer marked in Mother Graham's book—"Abide with me, Lord, for it is toward evening, and the day of this toilful life is now far spent."

The sense of time past and passing, standing still and moving on. Feeling and reflecting merged like the water, sky and land.

Most of all there was the sense of eternity which God has put in our hearts, and of which true rest in this life is a foretaste.

GOD AT REST

The psalmist tells us, "There is a river whose streams make glad the city of God" (Ps 46:4). I wonder: does God—did God—ever rest by his river?

At creation God rested the seventh day: the phrase from Genesis 2:2-3 could be translated "He enjoyed the seventh day."

God, being pure energy, does not need the rest of replenishment that we do, nor cleansing, though perhaps the environment did. Rather, his pure desire to love and enjoy his creation allowed him to stop and contemplate the beauty and goodness of what he had made, with no need to totally control it. He also gave his world breathing space.

A river nourished Eden and flowed from it (see Gen 2:10). Could we (allowing our imagination some space) imagine an incarnate God sitting by the river, drinking in great drafts of joy in the work he had finished, as an artist might sit and look and look at a finished painting? Was he in a playful mood as he watched the fish he had made jumping in the river he created?

Rest—and how can we ever express what "time" is for God?— was apparently a "day" fully present and enjoyed, in which creative work was finished, contemplated, enjoyed, and the future envisioned and anticipated. Did God catch his breath, so to speak, the breath of his creative spirit, not in weariness (for only the obstinacy of his rebel creation would later weary him) but in fulfillment and satisfaction?

Was this day of rest a pausing for the next even greater work of *re*-creation, a work that would take even greater effort, to rescue a creation gone off the tracks, a redemption to be finally consummated only in the vision of Revelation, where once again the river of life, clear as crystal, flows down the center of the city of God as it once did in the garden of God, and the dwelling of God is with his people forever?

So for us, made (and in Christ remade) in God's image, there remains a rest. In its essence, rest is more than leisure or napping or "time on our hands." God's rest for us involves freedom — to trust, to live out his dream for us, to work, create, play, let go and move on.

The rest God offers is the freedom to be fully present in the moment, free to reflect and enjoy what has been; to let go of the deficits and regrets that wear us down; free to envision what will be, what we are being re-created for; free to unburden ourselves of regretful thoughts about our yesterdays and anxious thoughts about our tomorrows.

During that stop at Dunkeld by the River Tay, I was hearing through the gentle murmur of the waters the words of Jesus, an invitation spoken so long ago, an offer now open if we are still enough to hear:

> Come to me, all you who are weary and burdened, and I will give you rest. Take my yoke upon me, and learn from me, for I am gentle and humble in heart, *and you will find rest for your souls.*

The memory of Dunkeld reminds me that I may not again make a trip to that river, but there is always time to stop and hear again those words from the river flowing within.

Practicing Attentiveness: Centering Prayer

Thomas Keating advocates "centering prayer" as a prayer of the heart. He recommends one or two daily periods in which we wait quietly in God's presence, perhaps repeating a "sacred word," and let go of our thoughts, neither holding on to them nor struggling with them. Here are a few of his descriptive sentences. "Centering prayer is not so much an exercise of attention as intention. . . . Centering prayer is not a way of turning on the presence of God. Rather, it is a way of saying, 'Here I am.' . . . The sacred word is not a means of going where you want to go. It only directs your intention toward God."

I have found it helpful both at the beginning and at the ending of a day to spend a few minutes in this kind of quietness, saying "My souls waits for the Lord," or "Be still and know that I am God." I suppose it is like a gentle knocking on God's door to say, "I am here, waiting."

One Who Paid Attention
Henri Nouwen, a Restless Prophet

THE WRITINGS OF THE LATE HENRI NOUWEN often speak to the condition of my own heart, and to countless others, not least because he so poignantly opened up his own inner struggles. Yet this man who ministered peace to many was himself a restless soul. His friend Parker Palmer recalls an experience with Nouwen at a retreat.

> I was conscious of being in the company of a world-class contemplative and I was expecting to have an extraordinary experience sitting next to him during worship. But as we sat . . . I realized that the bench was jiggling. I opened my eyes . . . and saw Henri's leg working furiously. . . . As time went on, the fidgeting got worse. I opened my eyes again only to find him checking his watch to see what time it was.

Sometimes Nouwen would become so desperate for companionship that after he spoke to an attentive crowd, if his hosts did not invite him out for a late supper he would go to his room and stay on the phone for hours calling friends in distant places.

In one of Nouwen's first books, he described the movement from restlessness to restfulness. There is first the admission of our being incomplete, the owning of our own pain. But then, he writes, we need to give up our illusions, our "Messianic expectations" that anything in this world will complete us. "To wait for moments or places where no pain exists, no separation is felt and where all human restlessness has turned into inner peace is waiting for a dream world."

What then is the cure for our restless souls? Not to move outward but to take the difficult road of conversion from loneliness to solitude. Can I sit still long enough for restlessness to turn into restfulness?

No wonder Nouwen could describe with such pathos the depth he found in Rembrandt's painting *The Return of the Prodigal*: he carried within him his own prodigal soul.

Nouwen himself learned to sit still in July 1986, when he went to the Hermitage in St. Petersburg to view Rembrandt's great painting, which he had longed to see firsthand after seeing it on a poster. He was so drawn in that a guard brought him a chair and he sat for four hours, gazing and making notes. He paid such close attention that he began to see it as "my personal painting, the painting that contained not only the heart of the story that God wants to tell me, but also the heart of the story that I want to tell. . . . All of the Gospel is there. All of my life is there. All of the lives of my friends is there."

Nouwen saw himself there as the younger runaway son, the stay-at-home older brother and the waiting Father. He also saw his own path home, from restlessness to rest: "This place had always been there. I had always been aware of it as the source of grace. But I had not been able to enter it and truly live there."

As he paid such close attention, the painting became "a mysterious window" through which he could step into the kingdom of God. "God himself showed me the way."

Grandfather Time

When Evening Comes

*Let it come, as it will, and don't
be afraid. God does not leave us
comfortless, so let evening come.*
JANE KENYON

*Time past and time future
What might have been and what has been
Point to one end, which is always present.*
T. S. ELIOT, "BURNT NORTON"
(FOUR QUARTETS)

*May the day go by joyously
In the morning of purity,
In the high noon of faith
And without nightfall upon the spirit.*
ST. AMBROSE

*I will lie down and sleep in peace;
   for you alone, O LORD,
   make me dwell in safety.*
PSALM 4:8 NIV

Then shall we know even as we are known.
ST. PAUL

Compline is the hour that signifies completion. As David Steindl-Rast explains, "Compline completes the circle of the day . . . connecting the end of the day with the end of life itself. It reinforces the theme that the rhythm of our days parallels the rhythm of our life, and the way we live each hour."

At Compline, bells call the community to bring the day to a proper close. There are prayers of confession, a time for examination of conscience, and then entering into night and sleep.

Darkness comes often as a threat, but it can also be a grace. Psalm 91, often sung at Compline, is a reminder that in the darkness we are sheltered under the wings of the Almighty. Compline is a time to return to the God who first formed us in our mother's womb, to rest, as Jesus pictured, like chicks under the wings of a mother hen, until morning comes.

So at the hour of Compline the last prayers of the day include the petition "A peaceful night and a perfect end grant us."

Evening comes to every day, every task, every phase, every relation, every life. As a day or a life come to a close, our most heartfelt questions may be *Am I safe? Am I loved? Do I have a true home in this universe?*

The coming of night can be very threatening. When our Debbie was small, she would take a flying leap into her bed because she was scared of what dark thing might be under it. From childhood on, the gathering darkness can trigger our fear of the unknown — both a darkness within and a darkness beyond.

So what does Compline signal? Only a conclusion, or a true completion? Merely an ending, or a lead-in to the Great End?

THE SOUND OF COMPLINE

Compline has a rich and round sound to it. The word seems to hold both layers of comfort and an underlying irony.

The comfort involves a sense of fulfillment. When I picture Compline, I see myself sitting by a blazing fire in the winter or on the porch of our daughter's mountain home in the summer, a drink or a book in my hand, simply gazing at the fire or the hills in fading light, enjoying a sense of well-being now that the busy day is over.

But there is a built-in irony in Compline. The word means "completion," yet is any day ever really complete? Over, yes—but complete, when there are always many loose ends that have not been tied up?

As for my life, even at the end of the day will it be fully completed? Life, says Rahner, is always an unfinished symphony. There are always so many things to remember and be grateful for, so many others to regret, to leave undone or still to do.

So Compline is a paradox. A day is always *complete* in the sense that it is over but always *incomplete* since there is more to do.

The poet Rainer Maria Rilke caught something of this mood:

I live my life in widening circles
that reach out across the world.
I may not complete this last one
but I give myself to it.

But still the thought nags me: will I complete this last circle? I know I can never finish it truly. In part that is because I myself am not yet at the end. I have passed my seventy-sixth birthday, but in my mind at least I am not yet "old." And since I have not passed through the whole process of aging, how can I look back and say: here is how I did it, here is what I learned?

To be honest, I hesitate because I do not much want to go there. Who wants to get old? Or to die, at least at an age that seems too early? These days many of our friends are getting ready to enter retirement homes. It is one of the last things *I* want to do.

Compline, as the end of a day, makes us reflect on many endings and turning points and many new roads for us to travel. It's not bad, of course, to think of the end of life even when we are younger. Indeed there are many "Compline times." Our oldest grandson, Graham, is in such a time, having just graduated from university and started his first full-time job. Compline time might be the ending of a job or a romantic relation, the leaving of a longtime home or the pause that we take as we enter into a new venture.

In my hesitation I sense kinship with Mary Morrison. In her later years she compared her entering into the next passage of life to what it was like when she became an adult: "The new road is not marked at all, and I am feeling my uncertainties strongly." So I am not alone in hesitating to enter, or even write about, the night journey.

If I find it difficult to put my thoughts of Compline in order, it is in part because this is the time when I want to pull together the threads of my life but also the time when they tend to get most unraveled, when the mysteries of birth and life and death press in.

I would like my life to be like one of those beautifully designed and intricate Celtic cords, where the strands weave intricately in and about each other and all are bound together. Yet I realize that the place of beginning—where the cord starts—is a mystery, as is the end: how will there be a final joining and completion?

Morrison's experience resonates again with me when she ruefully admits: "Every time I write persuasively and eloquently about something that I haven't experienced fully, life pulls me up short."

LIFE PULLS US UP SHORT

This came home to me most strongly several years ago. An older friend had told me to expect some physical breakdowns when I turned seventy, but I had smugly thought to myself that would not happen. Then life got my attention in very dramatic fashion.

Within a six-week period I found I had prostate cancer (early and treatable, and now undetectable) and then a major heart attack.

The heart "event" (as the doctors call it) came on a Wednesday night. After dinner with friends, I woke about 4 a.m. feeling a deep ache in my left shoulder and upper arm. A hot shower and aspirin did not help. Finally I roused my wife Jeanie and asked her to drive me to the hospital emergency room, where I was quickly taken to the "cath lab."

It was a profoundly unsettling experience to lie there watching my heart on the monitor with a probe snaking around it, to hear the calm voice of the doctor say "occluded." One of the main arteries that feeds the most important part of the heart was nearly 100 percent blocked. A balloon was used to make space in the artery, and a stent inserted to keep it open, and it has done so.

That quick action by my young cardiologist and disciplined rehab brought a full recovery of the heart ejection function. But during that heart episode and in the hours after, I was faced with my mortality as never before.

In the early hours after the attack, my doctor son-in-law Craig came to my intensive-care room. I can still see him kneeling by my bed and praying for my recovery. He read to me words from Isaiah 30:15, as I mentioned in chapter eight, and left them on a card by my bed:

In returning and rest is your salvation;
    in quietness and trust is your strength.

After Craig left, I was alone. Lying there I asked myself: *Suppose I were dying. What would I be sensing?* More than any time in my life I had to face the paradox of ending life but not completing it.

Here is what came to my mind in those reflective and painful moments: *If I died today, I would be very sad for all those I love I would be leaving behind, but I would also have a deep sense of gladness and thankfulness for the full life I have experienced.*

That comes as close as I can possibly express to what I hope and believe will be my deepest truth when my evening does finally come to a close, the desire

- to *complete* life—with gratitude for all that has been
- to leave life *incomplete*—with trust in the God who will always be

This is the paradox of Compline. Yet Compline should be—can be—a time to look back with gratitude and forward with trust, and to discern the True End of life in the light of eternity.

GRANDFATHER TIME

Cynthia Bourgeault recalls standing on a high island bluff off the coast of Maine. From it she could watch a ferry carry her daughter to the mainland to meet her boyfriend, the boyfriend's car coming down the landing road, her daughter moving to the front of the boat in excited anticipation.

That bluff became a powerful visual image. From Cynthia's vantage point it seemed as if every moment of this unfolding little drama was contained in one huge *now*. It was as if she could see all things coming together, as if time disappeared and became one. It reminded her of the ancient word *apokatastatis*—"restoration"—the word Peter used to speak of the time "for God to restore everything, as he promised long ago through his holy prophets" (Acts 3:21 NIV). She grasped how all times

> are contained in something bigger: a space that is none other than the Mercy itself. The fullness (or "end") of time becomes this space: a vast, gentle wideness in which all possible outcomes—all our little histories, past, present, and future; all our hopes and dreams—are already contained and, mysteriously, *already fulfilled.*

Grandfather Mountain in the Blue Ridge Mountains of North Carolina has become for me that high bluff, that visual image — the place of restoration and coming together, the "Compline" of things. Perhaps this is in part because I grew up near very flat farmlands in southern Ontario and high places near water have always had a special draw for my soul.

Grandfather is about two and a half hours from our home in Charlotte. When I make the trip, about halfway there I can begin to see the mass of peaks that make up the mountain chain. Only when I get closer and am passing through the tiny village of Foscoe does the grandfather image really appear. Suddenly he is there: the profile of an old man on his back, asleep on the ridge that is his mountain cot. His forehead, slightly crooked nose and stubborn chin are quite visible. All he lacks is a corncob pipe to be the image of a mountain man. One can almost imagine Daniel Boone traversing these hills on horseback and pausing to pass the time of day with this old fellow.

This mountain hovering over a small man-made lake is for me one of the "thin places" the ancient Celts spoke of, the edges of the world where heaven and earth seem very near each other. For many years and in many seasons with our family I have come here, have seen the place come brilliantly awake in morning sun, be shrouded in the fogs of afternoon or point toward the stars set like diamonds in a deep, dark winter sky.

There are many paths up to the top of Grandfather, where there is a swinging bridge that in high winds can be very scary. But while there are many paths, there is only one highest point: McRae Peak, from which on a very clear morning one can see the tallest buildings of Charlotte eighty miles away. For me the mountain is a parable: though we all long and look in different ways, the only truly worthy End of our longing and looking is the one true High God,

Father of the patriarchs, the prophets and our Lord Jesus Christ.

Grandfather Mountain speaks to me of evening time — and of recovery, accomplishment, restoration. After my heart "event" I went through some weeks of cardiac rehab. The first day, the director asked what my number-one goal for recovery was. Instantly I knew. "I want to lead the charge up Grandfather Mountain again," I said, remembering the many times I had led groups of young leaders up the steep ascent.

The climb up Grandfather is not especially difficult. It is more long and demanding. There are some tricky places where one can climb only by going up ladders strapped to the steep rocks and where some delicate balance is needed. The climb can bring on heavy breathing, sore legs and some moments of anxiety in crossing a rock face from one small ledge to another. But the view from the top is worth it.

A year and a half after the heart attack, I finally achieved my goal and with my young assistant Jonathan climbed all the way to the top. *Crawled* would be more true for the last part, as on hands and knees I drew myself on to McCrae Peak — one huge rock on the very top, one of the highest points east of the Rockies — and stood there watching the landscape stretch out for 360 degrees to the far horizons.

From the top I used my cell phone to call another young friend who had climbed to this place with me. When he answered at his home in Vancouver, a continent away, I said, "Ken, I am here. On Grandfather. I made it. And I want you to be my witness."

There was both exhaustion and ecstasy, the sense of being able just to look and take in what was there, not having to accomplish anything else, recalling the rolling times of day and of life, anticipating the coming together of light and darkness. For at dusk from below Grandfather would be a liminal space, where over the high peaks light and darkness would meet.

Grandfather is that kind of visual image. It recalls the One who is from everlasting to everlasting, the dwelling place of every generation, of every time and space of life, the One who appeared in glory to Moses on a mountain, whose presence transfigured his Son on yet another high place, and who now is transforming us into that same image.

ATTENDING TO OUR TRUE END

Our journey together through this book has been one of learning to pay attention to the "hours" of our lives, whether the hours of a single day or the stages of our lives.

To what then should we especially pay attention at Compline?

Mary Morrison in her wise way suggests that evening is when we can "turn from our long life of attending to others and begin to pay attention to ourselves" and become "artists in the understanding of our own lives."

I agree, with the proviso that now we seek to discern the hidden wholeness of our lives, not just the separate parts, and that we pay attention not so much to the ending as to the End. Now our attention is not so much to the way our life closes as to the purpose for which we were sent in the first place. So our attention to ourselves is not just about ourselves but about our True End.

This is the way T. S. Eliot used the word *end* in his masterful *Four Quartets*, not in the sense of termination but of purpose:

In my beginning is my end . . .
In my end is my beginning.

And again,

What we call the beginning is often the end
And to make an end is to make a beginning.

The end is where we start from.

Eliot understood that all times — time present, time past and perhaps time future — "point to one end, which is always present."

Or, as in the once well-known and not worn-out question of the Shorter Catechism:

What is the chief end of man?
Man's chief end is to glorify God and enjoy him forever.

Even better, as Jesus taught, the supreme end and blessing of the pure in heart is to see God (Mt 5:8).

WHAT IS DEEPEST IN ME?

That is the crucial question. Not what is longest — how many years I will have? But what is deepest — what am I made for? And always what is deepest (to use Frederick Buechner's words again) is *longing*: to long, for a long time, from a long way off, to belong, to come to my heart's eternal home.

In my mind I go back to two childhood memories, both of which spoke to my early imagination about what eternity means.

Not far from one of our houses was the city jail, a foreboding pile of gray stone. For some strange reason, at the front of the jail there was a huge boulder. My mother used it to try to give me some idea of how long eternity is.

"Imagine," she said, "that once every thousand years a little bird comes, takes one grain of that rock in its beak and flies off. By the time the rock is all gone, eternity will just have begun." The thought was quite astounding, but it did not help me to understand eternity except that it must be a very, very long time!

Then I recall picking up a shell from some seashore and holding it to my ear. In it I seemed to hear a voice, a soft and whistling sound, like the roar of distant waves, a call that seemed to come from some far-off place, not quite the sound of earth and sea though not foreign to me either, a voice that seemed to whisper to me that there was another world, mysterious but real.

Mystery is a word we find often in the Bible, in relation to life and death. "Listen," wrote Paul, "I will tell you a mystery! We will not all die, but we will all be changed" (1 Cor 15:51).

When the Bible writers employ the term *mystery*, they use it in a very special way, not like the mystery of a puzzle we cannot solve or a mystery novel with an ending we cannot guess. Rather, biblical "mystery" is a truth that is hidden to our natural eyes and reason, one that must be revealed and uncovered if we are to experience it. As Philip Toynbee wrote, "mysteries are not problems to be solved, but realities to be contemplated."

To quote Paul again: " 'What no eye has seen, nor ear heard, nor the human heart conceived, what God has prepared for those who love him' — these things God has revealed to us through the Spirit; for the Spirit searches everything, even the depths of God" (1 Cor 2:9-10).

And the mysterious realities that we long for above all are *the place to which we belong, the person to whom we belong and the persons we are becoming.*

A PLACE, THE PERSON AND REAL PERSONS

Jesus began to make these mysteries clear when he was getting ready to leave his disciples, who were anxious about what was going to happen to them. He described for them the life yet to be: "In my Father's house there are many dwelling places. If it were not so, would I have told you that I go to prepare a place for you? . . . I will come again and will take you to myself, so that where I am, there you may be also" (Jn 14:2-3).

Here are the two realities of heaven: place and personhood — a place to go and a person to be with: "where I am, there you may be."

When Jesus had finished speaking to them, he turned in prayer to his Father and said, "This is eternal life, that they may know you, the only true God, and Jesus Christ whom you have sent" (Jn 17:3). "Eternal life" on Jesus' terms means a different quality of life. It signifies not *duration*—how *long* we live—but *relation*, with *whom* we live: the only true God. And in knowing the one true God in Christ, we also come to know our own true selves.

As John Calvin said in the opening chapter of his great work *The Institutes of the Christian Religion:* "True and substantial wisdom principally consists of two parts, the knowledge of God, and the knowledge of ourselves."

This is the Great End. And this is the great wisdom which calls for our attention, at every hour but especially as we move into the last hour of our life and return again and again above all to find our true home and discover our most real identity. And as we do, as Paul wrote, "we will all be changed" (1 Cor 15:51).

The end of our lifelong journey and quest is not merely a change of location, as if some celestial moving van could take you and me and our stuff from our current address to a house in the sky. It involves a profound transformation, the emergence of our true self, so that in becoming like Christ we most truly become ourselves—at home in our skin and in our soul, as Irenaus said, "humans fully alive."

"Finding myself" is one of the catchphrases of pop psychology. Yet the desire to know ourselves truly is more than a passing fad. It has roots deep in ancient wisdom and the truth of creation, in the desire of the Creator that each created thing and person may, in being true to its own nature, fulfill God's creative intent.

The English poet Gerard Manley Hopkins crafted words that express this desire in one of my favorite poems, his magnificent "As

Kingfishers Catch Fire." Each mortal thing, he wrote, whether
kingfishers, dragonflies, or stones dropped in wells

> does one thing and the same:
> Deals out that being indoors each one dwells;
> Selves — goes itself, *myself* it speaks and spells,
> Crying *What I do is me: for that I came.*

This desire to be most truly ourselves shows up in those who as
they go are touched and changed by God's grace:

> For Christ plays in ten thousand places,
> Lovely in limbs, and lovely in eyes not his
> To the Father through the features of men's faces.

How utterly astounding! That Christ may be seen in the features of my face and yours! The Scripture gives shape and substance to this hope. God had this in mind from the beginning, Paul
tells us, and is using all that happens to us for this end: "We know
that all things work together for good for those who love God, who
are called according to his purpose. For those whom he foreknew
he also predestined to be conformed to the image of his Son, in order that he might be the firstborn within a large family" (Rom 8:28-
29).

Or as in a slightly different vein he wrote to the first believers at
Corinth: "All of us, with unveiled faces, seeing the glory of the Lord
as though reflected in a mirror, are being transformed into the same
image from one degree of glory to another; for this comes from the
Lord, the Spirit" (2 Cor 3:18).

When I think of the flaws I am only too conscious of in myself,
and what an inadequate image of Christ I must convey to others,
these words lift me. Paul did not write them to some ideal super-
saints. He wrote to people in the church at Corinth who by their
rivalry and selfishness had been showing anything but a positive

image of following Christ. In spite of their immaturity, Paul can say that his words apply to them too: "all of us . . . are being transformed."

Just imagine: the same glory which caused Moses' face to shine as he met God on Mount Sinai, the same glory which shone from the transfigured Christ on the mountain at Caesarea Philippi, can shine in and through you and me. And it can happen as we pay attention.

A transformation may be taking place in me—I trust so—but much of the time in my quotidian life it is not apparent. So how encouraging it is to know that Paul also understood that something is happening that may be hidden now: "You have died, and your life is hidden with Christ in God. When Christ who is your life is revealed, then you also will be revealed with him in glory" (Col 3:3-4).

How heartening to trust that what we are now is not the end: "Beloved, we are God's children now; what we will be has not yet been revealed. What we do know is this: when he is revealed, we will be like him, for we will see him as he is. And all who have this hope in him purify themselves, just as he is pure" (1 Jn 3:2-3).

One of our common fears as we get older is dissolution. Yet as the physical dissolves, I desire that what is essential—"the pattern of the glory," as Charles Williams calls it—will emerge. And this is not to happen only in some future state: it is promised as a daily renewing: "Even though our outer nature is wasting away, *our inner nature is being renewed day by day.* For this slight momentary affliction is preparing us for an eternal weight of glory beyond all measure" (2 Cor 4:16-17).

Several years ago I flew on short notice to England for a last visit with my dear friend Bishop A. Jack Dain, who for thirty years had been my mentor, confidant, adviser and spiritual father. Our visit was filled with loving and grateful reminiscence and strong hope. In his weakness I saw what his wife Hester remarked: "As he grows weaker, his essential sweetness is shining through more and more."

That is the "hidden wholeness" that Merton referred to, a wholeness that I long to be revealed to me, in me, day by day.

A TESTAMENT OF DESIRE

With a nod to the Quaker Thomas Kelly's *A Testament of Devotion*, I want at this time of life to set down my own *testament of desire*. And for that I can do no better than borrow the words of the psalmist:

> One thing I ask of the LORD,
>   this is what I seek:
> that I may dwell in the house of the LORD
>   all the days of my life,
> to gaze upon the beauty of the LORD
>   and to seek him in his temple. (Ps 27:4 NIV)

Like the psalmist, I desire not only to gaze on God's beauty in heaven but to catch transforming glimpses here and now.

I desire to become all that God created me to be.

I desire to live each moment as a human fully alive and redeemed.

I desire that Christ may be seen in the features of my face.

I desire that the "hidden wholeness" may be revealed in me.

I desire to know fully and to be known fully even as now I am fully known by God (1 Cor 13:12).

I desire that "the pattern of the glory" will emerge.

I desire glimpses of the glory even now—moments when glory seems to shine through, as in Revelation John saw in heaven "a door stood open!" (Rev 4:1).

I desire to have my imagination quickened with a preview of heaven.

I desire the clarity and centeredness that are marks of heaven—

where "the Lamb is at the center of the throne" (Rev 5:6 NIV) — to mark my life now.

I desire to be part of what will bring joy and glory to the Creator — the restoration of all things that is surely coming.

I desire to have a home for God in my heart and to come home each day, each hour, from now to eternity.

I desire to look with more and more attention until that longing for home becomes reality.

Practicing Attentiveness: Examen

When the bombs were falling on Europe during World War II, thousands of orphaned children were placed in refugee camps. There they were safe and fed. But since many of them had almost starved, they could not go to sleep at night: they feared that when they woke up they would have nothing to eat. At last someone came up with the idea of giving each child at bedtime a small portion of bread. They went to sleep holding it and thinking, *Tonight I had something to eat, and tomorrow I will eat again.*

The authors of *Sleeping with Bread* use this story to suggest ending the day with the "examen," asking two questions before sleep: For what moment today am I most grateful? For what moment am I least grateful? The questions can be phrased differently: Where did I sense God most today? Where did I miss him? Where was I most fulfilled? Most drained? Where was I the happiest? The saddest?

The examen is not a new practice. It was recommended by Ignatius in his *Spiritual Exercises*, because it helped to change him from a soldier to a pilgrim walking to Jerusalem. My wife and I have sometimes found it helpful (although she prefers not to remember the least happy moments at bedtime). It is a reminder to be grateful for the Bread of Life who sustains us at the ending and beginning hours of our lives.

One Who Paid Attention
Hwee Hwee Tan — Becoming What We Look At

HWEE HWEE TAN IS A WRITER who grew up in Singapore and now lives in New York. He writes of a time when he was burned out, after finishing the second draft of his second novel. Although he felt his work was going well, his personal life was falling apart.

For two years he had virtually shut himself off from friends, and consequently he was suffering from some separation anxiety and fear of intimacy. Even to pick up the phone to call a friend took a huge effort.

When he had a few weeks free from his writing projects, he decided to fly to Italy, a journey that became the most regenerative he had ever taken, creatively and spiritually.

In Italy he rediscovered the power of art and the way artists — imitators of God — can create beautiful things. "Beauty," Tan writes, "is anything . . . that stills the soul and fills it with joy, peace, and love." He gained a fresh vision of his own artistic gifts as an ability to bring healing.

He experienced such healing himself as he walked slowly through Rome, gazing at flowing fountains, unpredictably winding streets, beautifully designed buildings. In paying attention to beauty he was renewed.

> As I looked at those objects in Italy, the more beauty I saw, the more beautiful I felt inside. I began to understand a profound but simple truth: you become what you contemplate. In 2 Corinthians Paul writes that we, "beholding as in a mirror the glory of the Lord, are being transformed into the same image."

This verse uses the metaphor of God as mirror: God is a mirror at which we are told to gaze, and in the mirror we see ourselves, yet at the same time not ourselves, but God. As we look into the face of God, we become transformed. After gazing at the mirror face of God long enough, we see ourselves, having ourselves become images of God. When we gaze at the glorious, we become glorious. We become an image of what we look at.

Hwee Hwee Tan concludes: "That's the profound truth: you are what your mind looks at. You are what you contemplate."

Epilogue
The Journey Home

Our son Kevin and his wife Caroline were visiting us after Christmas with their daughter Anabel, age two and a half. On New Year's Eve I began to think about my "hopes and dreams" for the next year. I went to sleep on the sofa reading, woke at midnight to greet the new year sleepily and nodded off again.

In the morning, my new Australian Cattle Dog Wrangler came in as I was dozing to let me know it was time to be with him. Kevin was already up reading and motioned to me to be quiet so Anabel would not wake early. But then he made a noise in the bathroom next to where she was sleeping. In a moment Anabel appeared with her blanket, ragged stuffed rabbit and sleepy eyes.

"Oh no, I was afraid of this," Kevin moaned, thinking how tired she would be later in the day. "Any noise nearby wakes her up."

Anabel pulled a Siberian fox pelt off the sofa and held it close. "Do you want to sleep with Gagi for a while?" I asked.

She answered with a sleepy yes. So Anabel and Wrangler and I went to her room. She and I pulled the covers over us, and Wrangler settled on the floor.

I lay there without moving, and so did she. I am sure she thought she was helping Gagi to go back to sleep. As I listened to her little sleepy sounds and watched her as her eyes opened and closed, I wondered what a two-and-a-half-year-old thinks about when she lies in bed. When she is my age, might she still remember this morning time with Gagi?

Because I have very few memories of my own early years, I was surprised when there came to my mind a picture of Miss Thomas, the former missionary who invited me to ask Jesus into my heart when I was five. Suddenly I had the image of a very large, very pleasant lady wearing a cloth coat with a fur around her neck as was the style in those days, topped off with a feathered hat. Anabel, it seems, was helping me recover some childhood pictures.

Then my mind turned again toward my hopes and dreams for the coming year, but even more inwardly toward the preciousness of this moment with this beautiful child. I wanted it to go on. And on and on and on.

At last Anabel stirred, sat up and began to "read" *Frosty the Snowman* (whom she called Frosty the Snow Ma'am). Wrangler poked his head over the edge of the bed. "Do you want to go see Daddy?" I asked.

"Yes," Anabel said eagerly, and so we all got up for the first day of the new year.

A bit later I sipped coffee and read from the last movement of Eliot's *Four Quartets*. In the beauty of those moments, wondering about Anabel's thoughts, my own thoughts began to come clear and I began to understand a portion of Eliot's great poem more deeply. I remembered that at the very end Eliot writes of a Love that draws, a Voice that calls. And then come the words I cited in my introduction:

We shall not cease from exploration
And the end of all our exploring
Will be to arrive where we started
And know the place for the first time.

Eliot recalls moments when past and present became one, including (at the very beginning of his poem) the memory of going through a gate into a rose garden and hearing the voices of "children in the apple tree"—voices not known then but heard now.

Eliot's memory of the rose garden and children's voices shows us that in moments of intense experience there is revealed to us what can exist "here, now, always," if we follow down the path of humility. Time is redeemed when memory of the past and desire for the future are joined by love in the present.

Those words came as a flash of insight, with a force that grasped me deep within. They spoke of my calling for the year to come. When I was in high school and college I was probably old for my years, but now at this stage I sense I am rather young for my years. It is as if time were being compressed into another dimension.

Yet for us, in time, things always come to an end.

For Anabel, the time came to get ready to go to the airport for the trip home. She pitched a fit, crying, kicking and resisting. Caroline was mystified: she hadn't acted up like that in weeks.

While Anabel was being calmed down, I retreated outside to take Wrangler on his morning walk and drank in the quiet of the first morning of the year. As I did, my thoughts circled and centered.

What do I know that I know, not just what comes from others but that which is most truly from my deepest self? I asked myself.

As I walked the closing lines of May Sarton's "Now I Become Myself" came to me:

Now there is time, and Time is young.
O, in this single hour I live
All of myself and do not move.
I the pursued, who madly ran,
Stand still, stand still, and stop the sun.

I am learning truly to be myself, I thought, and what it means that (in Paul's words, Gal 2:20) "for me to live is Christ." This is the journey home to my own heart—the holy longing—and this is what I have been writing about, the purpose-drawn life. And the purpose that draws us is Love.

Being with Anabel that morning had called me back to long-hidden desires planted in my heart in childhood, now growing to become the song.

When the missionary lady Miss Thomas wrote letters, each closed with a citation of Romans 8:28, those unforgettable words of Paul about knowing that "in all things God works for the good of those who love him, who have been called according to his purpose . . . to be conformed to the likeness of his Son" (Rom 8:28-29 NIV). The destination is Christlikeness. The wonder is not only that we will be like him but that when we are like him we will most truly be ourselves. And as we make the journey from the groans of creation and the groaning of our own present lives (Rom 8:22-23), we also know that nothing in all creation "will be able to separate us from the love of God that is in Jesus Christ our Lord" (Rom 8:39).

So the mystery—the "still point in a turning world"—is opened to us not in the memory of time past or the desire of time future, neither in the vain attempt to clutch what passes nor in trying to achieve what is beyond our grasp, but as we live in the present in the presence of God's constant and unconquerable love.

Eliot's conclusion came to him from the voices of children in an apple tree. For me, it came in the presence and departure of Anabel.

When I came in from my walk, she was dressed and adorable in her little traveling outfit. Only a few minutes were left before they had to leave for the airport.

"Do you want to take a walk with Gagi and Wrangler?" I asked.

"Yes." She was quite clear she did.

So she took my hand, and the two of us and Wrangler walked down the back steps and onto the sidewalk. We passed the house and came to the front driveway, and I started toward the car.

"No," she protested, "walk."

So we walked. On to the corner, down the side street.

At that moment her daddy came out of the house and called for her. Instantly she cried out, "No, walk!" and ran up the street as fast as she could.

Kevin ran after her. She ran even faster, beginning to sob.

When he finally caught her and picked her up, she wailed and kicked and flailed. "Walk, walk," she cried, "Wrangler and Gagi!"

Kevin got her into her car seat, but I will not forget the tears that stained her flushed cheeks, the desolate look, the cries as they pulled out of the driveway.

Her visit was too short. Far too short. For her. For us.

I could not go back in the house. I sat on the front steps, Wrangler by my side, tears welling in my own eyes.

Through the glad voices of the children in the apple tree and the brokenhearted voice of my granddaughter in her car seat, through all these voices that call us to pay attention, Love is seeking us, the only Love that redeems time, that takes the fragments of what is past and the hope of what is coming and binds them together in the "love of God which is in Jesus Christ our Lord."

That love is reaching out even now, calling us to our heart's true home.

Appendix

Observing the Hours

IT HAS BEEN HELPFUL TO ME to have certain prayers to use at different "hours" of the day, prayers which speak to and from my own heart, prayers which aid me in carrying on a "continual conversation" with God—or, to be quite honest, a conversation which is often interrupted and must be restarted. These come from a variety of sources across the ages and are a personal selection of prayers that have helped me to be recalled to attentiveness. Those in bold type at the beginning of each hour are the ones I most often use. I offer these prayers as a small gift hoping they may also encourage you to find prayers which most truly represent your own innermost thoughts to God. They are not meant to prescribe a set way of praying but to be a stimulus for your heart's response to God who says, "Seek my face." And I offer them remembering also that C. S. Lewis wisely wrote that the prayer preceding all prayers should be: "May it be the real I who speaks. May it be the real Thou that I speak to."

VIGILS

**When I awake,
I am still with you.**
PSALM 139:18 NIV

I think of you on my bed,
    and meditate on you in the watches of the night.
PSALM 63:6

I bless the LORD who gives me counsel;
  in the night also my heart instructs me.
PSALM 16:7

LAUDS

O LORD, in the morning you hear my voice;
  in the morning I plead my case to you, and watch.
PSALM 5:3

This is the day that the LORD has made;
  let us rejoice and be glad in it.
PSALM 118:24

"Come," my heart says, "seek his face!"
  Your face, LORD, do I seek.
PSALM 27:8

Thou, the brightness of th'eternal glory,
Unto Thee is my heart, though without a word,
And my silence speaketh unto Thee.
JOHN WESLEY

The Lord God has given me
  the tongue of a teacher,
that I may know how to sustain
  the weary with a word.
Morning by morning he wakens —
  wakens my ear
  to listen as those who are taught.
ISAIAH 50:4

New *every morning* is your love, great God of light,
and *all day* long you are working for good in the world.
Stir up in us desire to serve you,

to live peacefully with our neighbors,
and to devote *each ∂ay* to your Son, our Savior,
  Jesus Christ the Lord.
THE WORSHIPBOOK: SERVICES AND HYMNS (WESTMINSTER PRESS)

Lord Jesus Christ, Son of God, have mercy upon me, a sinner.
THE JESUS PRAYER

Each one is a gift, no doubt,
mysteriously placed in your waiting hand
or set upon your forehead
moments before you open your eyes.
BILLY COLLINS, "DAYS"

Thanks,
thanks to you,
most high eternal Father,
for showing us today—
madly in love as you are with your creature—
. . . how your bride, your holy church,
can be reformed.
O eternal Trinity, mad with love.
CATHERINE OF SIENA

PRIME

To you, O LORD, I lift up my soul.
O my God, in you I trust. . . .
Make me to know your ways, O LORD;
  teach me Your paths.
Lead me in your truth, and teach me,
  for you are the God of my salvation;
  for you I wait all day long.
PSALM 25:1-2, 4-5

The arms of God be around my shoulders,
the touch of the Holy Spirit upon my head,
the sign of Christ's cross upon my forehead,
the sound of the Holy Spirit in my ears,
the fragrance of the Holy Spirit in my nostrils,
the vision of heaven's company in my eyes,
the conversation of heaven's company on my lips,
the work of God's church in my hands,
the service of God and the neighbor in my feet,
a home for God in my heart,
and to God, the Father of all, my entire being.
Amen.
ST. FURSEY

TERCE
We do our work for Jesus, with Jesus, to Jesus.
And that's what keeps it simple.
MOTHER TERESA

Breathe on me, breath of God,
Fill me with life anew.
EDWIN HATCH

SEXT
He gives power to the faint,
    and strengthens the powerless.
Even youths will faint and be weary,
    and the young will fall exhausted;
but those who wait for the LORD shall renew their strength,
    they shall mount up with wings like eagles,
they shall run and not be weary,
    they shall walk and not faint.

NONE
Therefore,
Let nothing hinder us,
Nothing separate us,
Nothing come between us.
Wherever we are,
In every place,
At every hour,
At every moment of the day,
Everyday and continually,
Let all of us . . .
Hold in our heart and love,
Honor, adore, serve,
Praise and bless,
Glorify and exalt,
Magnify and give thanks.
FRANCIS OF ASSISI

O give thanks to the LORD, for he is good;
   his steadfast love endures forever!
PSALM 118:1

VESPERS
Be at rest once more, O my soul,
   for the LORD has been good to you.
PSALM 116:7

My soul magnifies the Lord,
   and my spirit rejoices in God my Savior.
LUKE 1:46-47

COMPLINE
The Lord Almighty grant us a peaceful night and a perfect end.
Amen.

Guide us waking, O Lord, and guard us sleeping; that awake we may watch with Christ, and asleep we may rest in peace.
FROM AN ORDER FOR COMPLINE,
BOOK OF COMMON PRAYER

Lord Jesus, stay with us, for evening is at hand and the day is past; be our companion in the way, kindle our hearts, and awaken hope, that we may know thee as thou art revealed in Scripture and the breaking of the bread. Grant this for the sake of thy love. Amen.
FROM DAILY EVENING PRAYER: RITE TWO,
BOOK OF COMMON PRAYER

Keep watch, dear Lord, with those who work, or watch, or weep this night, and give your angels charge over those who sleep. Tend the sick, Lord Christ; give rest to the weary, bless the dying, soothe the suffering, pity the afflicted, shield the joyous; and all for your love's sake. Amen.
FROM AN ORDER FOR COMPLINE,
BOOK OF COMMON PRAYER

I will lie down and sleep in peace,
    for you alone, O Lord,
    make me dwell in safety.
PSALM 4:8 NIV

May God support us all the day long
Till the shadows lengthen
and the busy world is hushed
and the fever of life is done.
Then, in God's mercy
May God grant us a safe lodging,
and a holy rest
and peace at last.
JOHN HENRY CARDINAL NEWMAN

Circle me, Lord
Keep protection near
And danger afar

Circle me, Lord
Keep hope within
Keep doubt without

Circle me, Lord
Keep light near
And darkness afar

Circle me, Lord
Keep peace within
Keep evil out

A Celtic prayer. Words by David Adam. Design by Susanna Morse. Used by permission.

Notes

An Introduction

pp. 10-11   Annie Dillard's fish-stalking: Annie Dillard, *Pilgrim at Tinker Creek* (New York: HarperPerennial, 1974), pp. 184-86.

p. 11   "We shall not cease from exploration": T. S. Eliot, *Four Quartets* (New York: Harcourt and Brace, 1943), p. 59.

pp. 11-12   "The sand trap and the clouds . . .": Walker Percy, *Love in the Ruins* (New York: Avon Books, 1971), p. 20.

p. 12   "absolute attention": Simone Weil, *Waiting for God* (New York: Harper & Row, 1951), p. 71.

p. 13   "Old men ought to be explorers": Eliot, *Four Quartets*, p. 32.

p. 15   "To say that holiness is a fish": Dillard, *Pilgrim at Tinker Creek*, p. 186.

p. 16   "Looking along the beam": C. S. Lewis, "Meditation in a Toolshed," in *God in the Dock* (Grand Rapids, Mich.: Eerdmans, 1970), pp. 212-15.

Chapter 1: Paying Attention

p. 21   These hours were not a ritual: Explaining the "canonical hours" which became a part of this Rule, Benedict wrote:

> As the Prophet saith: "Seven times a day have I given praise to Thee," this sacred sevenfold number will be fulfilled by us in this wise if we perform the duties of our service at the time of Lauds, Prime, Tierce, Sext, None, Vespers, and Complin; because it was of these day hours that he hath said: "Seven times a day I have given Praise to Thee." For the same Prophet saith of the night watches "At midnight I arose to confess to Thee." At these times, therefore, let us offer praise to our Creator "for the judgments of His justice;" namely, at Lauds, Prime, Tierce, Sext, None, Vespers, and Complin; and let us rise at night to praise Him. (quoted in <www.kensmen.com/catholic/hours.html>)

David Steindl-Rast has described Benedict's hours as a kind of trellis or lattice that is meant to support our daily lives in much the same way as flowering plants grow on a trellis. It's well worth reading his book *Music of Silence: A Sacred Journey Through the Hours of the Day* (Berkeley, Calif.: Seastone, 1998) for an intriguing discussion of the "canonical hours."

p. 21   in fact Benedict wrote his Rule for laypeople: "My words . . . are addressed to thee, whoever thou art, that, renouncing thine own will, dost put on the strong and bright armour of obedience in order to fight for the Lord Christ, our true King." Benedict, quoted in "St. Benedict of Nursia," in *The Catholic Encyclopedia*, <www.newad vent.org/cathen/02467b.htm>, accessed May 30, 2007.

p. 22   "not a numerical measure . . . but a soul measure": Steindl-Rast, *Music of Silence*, p. 3.

p. 24   "Blessed are the clear at center": The "clear at center" rendering is suggested by F. Dale Bruner, *Matthew: A Commentary* (Dallas: Word, 1987), 1:148.

p. 26   "For prayer is awakeness": Douglas Steere, *Prayer in the Contemporary World* (Wallingford, Penn.: Pendle Hill Publications, 1990), pp. 4-5.

p. 26   "The Powers of Ten" is produced by Molecular Expressions and may be found online at <micro.magnet.fsu.edu/primer/java/scienceopticsu/powersof10>, accessed May 30, 2007.

p. 27   the belief that science rules out God: Diogenes Allen, for many years professor of the philosophy of religion at Princeton Theological Seminary, told me that when he was a graduate student in philosophy at Princeton University a half-century ago, *God* was a word never heard in the discussions in the philosophy lounge, unless in joking or cursing. "Now," he said, "that's changed. And God is the subject of intense discussion." In his book *Christian Belief in a Postmodern World* (Louisville, Ky.: Westminster John Knox, 1989), Allen says that "not only are the barriers to Christian belief erected by the modern mentality collapsing, but . . . philosophy and science, once used to undermine belief in God, are now seen in some respects as actually pointing toward God" (p. 2).

p. 28   "A breakthrough of hope": Bilquis Sheikh, "Beginning in Ourselves: Narrative," in *The Lord of the Journey: A Reader in Christian Spirituality*, ed. Roger Pooley and Philip Seddon (London: Collins Liturgical, 1986), pp. 90-91.

p. 32   the sun rises over and over: G. K. Chesterton, *Orthodoxy* (New York: Image Books, 1990), p. 60.

p. 35   "all-seeing eye": Simon Tugwell, *Prayer: Living with God* (Springfield, Ill.: Templegate, 1975), pp. 24-25.

p. 35   "selective inattention and forgetting": Marshall Jenkins, *A Wakeful Faith: Spiritual Practice in the Real World*, quoted in a review in *Weavings: A Journal of the Christian Spiritual Life*, July-August 2002, p. 47.

p. 37   "to be 'lost in wonder' ": Esther De Waal, *Lost in Wonder: Rediscovering the Spiritual Art of Attentiveness* (Collegeville, Minn.: Liturgical, 2003). The title is from the hymn "Love Divine, All Loves Excelling." This small treasure of a book offers ways to "retreat" in the various aspects of paying attention to God.

p. 37   "surprised by joy": C. S. Lewis, *Surprised by Joy: The Shape of My Early Life* (London: Fontana, 1955).

p. 37   "Simple attention to the present": Mary Morrison, *Let Evening Come: Reflections on Aging* (New York: Bantam Books, 1998), p. 70, quoted in De Waal, *Lost in Wonder*, p. 60.

p. 37   "If one looks long enough": May Sarton, *Journal of a Solitude* (New York: W. W. Norton, 1973), p. 99.

p. 38   "there lives the dearest freshness": Gerard Manley Hopkins, "God's Grandeur."

p. 38   "The art of awareness of God": Abraham J. Heschel, *Man Is Not Alone: A Philosophy of Religion* (New York: Farrar, Straus & Young, 1951), p. 88.

p. 39   "I think it's also a fair description of the writing process": Kathleen Norris, *The Cloister Walk* (New York: Berkley/Riverhead, 1996), pp. 142-43.

pp. 39-40   "We may ignore, but we can nowhere evade": C. S. Lewis, *Letters to Malcolm*, letter 73, quoted in Alan Jacobs, *The Narnian* (San Francisco: HarperCollins, 2005), p. 293.

p. 40   "always buried in thought": Quoted in Sylvia Nasar, *A Beautiful Mind* (New York: Touchstone, 1998). See especially chapter 5, "Genius."

p. 41   For a helpful account of how our Myers-Briggs types may affect our spiritual path and practices—both positively and negatively—I recommend Robert Mulholland's *Invitation to a Journey: A Road Map for Spiritual Direction* (Downers Grove, Ill.: InterVarsity Press, 1993). In chapter 7 Mulholland points out that for the

Senser the path of service comes easily, but for wholeness the Senser needs to cultivate awareness, while for the Intuiter awareness comes naturally but serving needs to be cultivated.

p. 41-42   "At first, it appears that nothing could be easier than seeing": James Elkins, *The Object Stares Back: On the Nature of Seeing* (New York: Simon & Schuster, 1996), p. 11.

p. 43   "I do not know where or how" and further quotes: Agnes Cunningham, "Alive to God in Christ Jesus," *Weavings*, July-August 2002, pp. 29-36.

p. 44   "No one lasts in the desert": "One must keep an eye out for landmarks, the position of the sun in the sky, tracks in the sand, threatening clouds. But equally important is staying attuned to one's inner condition—the progress of fatigue, the irritation of blisters, the forgetfulness to which the mind is prone, the slow rise of panic at the fear of being lost. The desert fathers and mothers spoke often of this attentiveness as *agrupnia*, the spiritual discipline of 'wakefulness,' the crucial importance of being aware, paying attention." Belden Lane, "Desert Attentiveness, Desert Indifference: Countercultural Spirituality in the Desert Fathers and Mothers," *Cross-Currents* 44, no. 2 (1994): 193-206.

p. 48   "when the presence came": Simone Weil, *Waiting for God* (New York: G. P. Putnam's Sons, 1951), p. 24.

p. 49   "with absolute attention": ibid., pp. 71-72.

p. 49   "the Our Father contains all possible petitions": ibid., p. 227.

p. 49   "Even if our efforts of attention": ibid., p. 59.

p. 49   "Nothing among human things": ibid., p. 74.

Chapter 2: The Birthing Hour

p. 51   "The Hour of Vigils is also a symbol of the waking up": David Steindl-Rast, *Music of Silence: A Sacred Journey Through the Hours of the Day* (Berkeley, Calif.: Seastone, 1998), pp. 23, 27.

p. 53   "The issue . . . is not so much the question": Alan Jones, *Passion for Pilgrimage: Notes for the Journey Home* (New York: Morehouse, 2000), p. 84.

pp. 62-63   Vincent Donovan's story comes from Vincent J. Donovan, *Christianity Rediscovered* (London: SCM Press, 1982), pp. 44-46, 62-63.

Chapter 3: Daybreak

p. 69   the discipline of "school studies": "The key to a Christian con-

ception of studies is the realization that prayer consists of attention. It is the orientation of all the attention of which the soul is
capable toward God. School children and students who love
God should never say: 'For my part I like mathematics'; 'I like
French'; 'I like Greek.' They should learn to like all these subjects because all of them develop that faculty of attention which,
directed toward God, is the very substance of prayer." Simone
Weil, *Waiting for God* (New York: G. P. Putnam's Sons, 1951), p.
106.

p. 75   "What do you believe in?": In *The Language of God: A Scientist Presents Evidence for Belief* (New York: Free Press, 2006), Francis
Collins not only tells the story of his spiritual journey but explains
how he finds his way through the challenge of relating his science
with his faith.

p. 77   "Prayer Is like Watching for the Kingfisher": Ann Lewin, quoted
in Esther De Waal, *Lost in Wonder: Rediscovering the Spiritual Art of
Attentiveness* (Collegeville, Minn.: Liturgical, 2003), p. 139.

p. 77   Prayer of John Wesley: Quoted in *The Joy of the Saints: Spiritual
Readings Throughout the Year,* ed. Robert Llewelyn (Springfield,
Ill.: Templegate, 1988), p. 189.

p. 78   "The prayer preceding all prayers": C. S. Lewis, *Letters to Malcolm, Chiefly on Prayer* (New York: Harcourt, Brace & World,
1964).

Chapter 4: Prime Time

p. 81   "the drum roll of the day": David Steindl-Rast, *Music of Silence: A
Sacred Journey Through the Hours of the Day* (Berkeley, Calif.: Seastone, 1998), pp. 51-52.

p. 82   "the voice of this calling": T. S. Eliot, *Four Quartets* (New York:
Harcourt and Brace, 1943), p. 59.

p. 83   "the true mystics of the quotidian": Kathleen Norris, *The Quotidian Mysteries* (New York: Paulist, 1998), p. 70.

p. 84   "It has nothing to do with whether": Eugene H. Peterson, *Eat
This Book: A Conversation in the Art of Spiritual Reading* (Grand
Rapids: Eerdmans, 2006), pp. 112-13.

p. 84   "wordless openness to the world": David Benner, "Being with
God: The Practice of Contemplative Prayer," *Conversations* 4, no.
2 (2006): 9.

pp. 85-86   the current interest in "spirituality": Robert Wuthnow, *After*

Heaven: Spirituality in America Since the 1950s (Berkeley: University of California Press, 1998).

p. 88   "The gracious indwelling of God": Lesslie Newbigin, *The Light Has Come: An Exposition of the Fourth Gospel* (Grand Rapids: Eerdmans, 1982), p. 196.

p. 88   "Inwardly, it is a ceaseless orientation": David Rensberger, "Persistence in Presence," *Weavings,* March-April 2007, p. 22.

p. 90   "This strange notion of indwelling": This material on Polanyi and Torrance comes from Andrew Witmer, ed., *Tacit Knowing and Truthful Knowing: The Life and Thought of Michael Polanyi,* audiotape, prod. Ken Myers (Charlottesville, Va.: Mars Hill Audio, 1999).

p. 91   "[Abiding] is the continually renewed decision": Newbigin, *Light Has Come,* p. 197.

pp. 92-93   "[Prayer] can only become unceasing prayer": Henri Nouwen with Michael J. Christensen and Rebecca J. Laird, *Spiritual Direction: Wisdom for the Long Walk of Faith* (San Francisco: HarperOne, 2006), pp. 61-62.

p. 93   Prime should be the time of listening first not to my needs and wants: I highly recommend Eugene Peterson's *Eat This Book.* Peterson is concerned that the contemporary enormous interest in spirituality is not matched by an equal interest in the Bible. "An interest in souls divorced from an interest in Scripture leaves us without a text that shapes these souls," he notes. He warns against the tendency to replace the Trinity of the Father, Son and Holy Spirit with "the Trinity of my Holy Wants, my Holy Needs, and my Holy Feelings." Peterson, *Eat This Book,* pp. 17, 31.

p. 95   "love that consists in this": Rainer Maria Rilke, *Letters to a Young Poet* (New York: W. W. Norton, 1993), p. 59.

p. 96   *Lectio divina* is an ancient practice: Peterson has an excellent presentation of *lectio divina* in chapter 7 of *Eat This Book.*

p. 97   "Prayer in all its forms is nothing more": Benner, "Being with God," pp. 6-12.

Chapter 5: Active Life

p. 101   "In a world where there is a wealth of information": Ken Mehlman, quoted in Joyce Purnick, "The 2004 Campaign: The Overview; One-Doorbell-One-Vote Tactic Re-emerges in Bush-Kerry Race," *New York Times,* April 6, 2004.

pp. 102-3   "continuous partial attention" and following material: Thomas
               Friedman quotes Linda Stone and provides his own analysis in
               "Cyber-Serfdom," in Thomas Friedman, *Longitudes and Attitudes:
               Exploring the World After September 11* (New York: Farrar, Strauss
               & Giroux, 2002), pp. 17-18. I also quote from Friedman's book
               The Lexus and the Olive Tree (New York: Anchor Books, 2000), p.
               10.

p. 105   Bruce Chatwin's learning experience in the Slow World is dis-
               cussed in Belden C. Lane, *The Solace of Fierce Landscapes: Explor-
               ing Desert and Mountain Spirituality* (New York: Oxford Univer-
               sity Press, 1998), pp. 9-10.

p. 111   "Spirituality is all about seeing": Juliet Benner, "O Taste and See:
               A Meditation on Rembrandt's *Return of the Prodigal Son*," *Conver-
               sations* 1, no. 2, Fall 2003, p. 59.

p. 112   Larry McMurtry's book about roads is *Roads: Driving America's
               Great Highways* (New York: Simon & Schuster, 2000).

p. 113   "Often we consider one or two points and jump to the next": An-
               thony Bloom, *Living Prayer* (Springfield, Ill.: Templegate, 1966),
               pp. 55.

p. 114   Søren Kierkegaard's parables can be found in Vernard Eller, *The
               Simple Life: The Christian Stance Toward Possessions, as Taught by
               Jesus, Interpreted by Kierkegaard* (Grand Rapids: Eerdmans,
               1973), pp. 82-83.

Chapter 6: The Noonday Demon

p. 116   "the hour of fervor and commitment": David Steindl-Rast, *Music
               of Silence: A Sacred Journey Through the Hours of the Day* (Berkeley,
               Calif.: Seastone, 1998), p. 70.

p. 116   "We are often susceptible": Deborah Smith Douglas, "Staying
               Awake," *Weavings* 17, no. 4 (July/August 2002): 39.

p. 117   Howard Gardner writes of multiple intelligences in *Multiple In-
               telligences: New Horizons in Theory and Practice* (New York: Basic
               Books, 2006).

p. 119   Denise Levertov poem: "Witness," in Denise Levertov, *Selected
               Poems* (New York: New Directions, 2002), p. 181.

p. 120   Psychologist Archibald Hart has written of stress in *The Hidden
               Link Between Adrenalin and Stress* (Waco, Tex.: Word, 1986), p. 59.

pp. 120-21   "a sense of apathy about all things in the world": Jason Read,
               quoted in Jill Lieber, "Read Emerges from Nightmare with

Stronger Faith, Will," *USA Today,* July 21, 2004, <www.usatoday
.com/sports/olympics/athens/boat/2004-07-21-rowing-read_x
.htm>, accessed May 31, 2007.

p. 122   "sin of the long haul": Douglas, "Staying Awake," pp. 39-40.

p. 123   "forget or refuse to go": Levertov, "Witness."

p. 124   "anything that destroys this attention": Douglas Steere, *Prayer in the Contemporary World* (Wallingford, Penn.: Pendle Hill Publications, 1990), p. 291.

p. 125   Gerald May's thoughts on addictions as attachments come from *Addiction and Grace: Love and Spirituality in the Healing of Addictions* (San Francisco: HarperSanFrancisco, 1988), pp. 3-4.

p. 126   "I have just ten seconds": Harold Abrahams is quoted in *Chariots of Fire,* dir. Hugh Hudson (Enigma Productions, 1981).

p. 128   "the constancy of God's love": Robert Llewelyn, *Julian Then and Now: The Mercy and Forgiveness of God,* Annual Julian Lecture (Norwich, U.K.: Friends of Julian of Norwich, 1997), p. 3.

p. 128   "Grace means there is nothing": Philip Yancey, *What's So Amazing About Grace?* (Grand Rapids: Zondervan, 1997), p. 70.

p. 130   "Ruthlessly eliminate hurry": John Ortberg, *The Life You've Always Wanted,* expanded ed. (Grand Rapids: Zondervan, 2002), pp. 76-77.

Holy Stillness

p. 136   Alice Fryling's *The Art of Spiritual Listening* (Colorado Springs: Waterbrook, 2003), pp. 75-76.

p. 137   "O, in this single hour": May Sarton, "Now I Become Myself," in *Selected Poems of May Sarton* (New York: Norton, 1978), p. 191.

pp. 138-39   Susan Howatch's novels about British clergy include *Glittering Images* (New York: Alfred A. Knopf, 1987); *Glamorous Powers* (New York: Alfred A. Knopf, 1988); *Ultimate Prizes* (New York: Alfred A. Knopf, 1989); *Scandalous Risks* (New York: Alfred A. Knopf, 1990); *Mystical Paths* (New York: Alfred A. Knopf, 1992); *Absolute Truths* (New York: Alfred A. Knopf, 1994).

Chapter 7: When Shadows Come

p. 141   "we encounter the reality that things don't last forever": David Steindl-Rast, *Music of Silence: A Sacred Journey Through the Hours of the Day* (Berkeley, Calif.: Seastone, 1998), p. 82.

p. 143   "The true religions of America are optimism and denial": Anonymous source, quoted in Kathleen Norris, *The Cloister Walk* (New

York: Riverhead, 1996), p. 94.

p. 144   "Reflecting on God's promise to write 'upon' our hearts": Deborah Smith Douglas, "Wounded and Healed," *Weavings*, March-April 2000, p. 23.

p. 146   "what we do with desire": Ronald Rolheiser, *The Holy Longing: The Search for a Christian Spirituality* (New York: Doubleday, 1999), p. 142.

p. 146   The paschal mystery, as Rolheiser describes it: Ibid., p. 145.

pp. 146-47   Rolheiser points out five distinct moments in the paschal cycle in ibid., p. 147.

p. 147   "Jesus gave the disciples forty days": Ibid., p. 153.

p. 148   Rolheiser's five steps for making the paschal mystery personal are from ibid., p. 148.

p. 149   "We have lifted the weight and instead of being crushed": Helen Luke, *Old Age: Journey into Simplicity* (New York: Bell Tower, 1987), p. 129.

p. 153   "to see everything against an infinite horizon": Ronald Rolheiser, *Against an Infinite Horizon* (New York: Crossroad, 1995).

pp. 155-56   "The first task in any love": Ibid., p. 58.

p. 158   "The love of Christ has no border": Alexander Whyte, *Lord, Teach Us to Pray* (Vancouver, B.C.: Regent College Publishing, 1998), pp. 154-55.

p. 160   Thomas Keating recommends a practice he calls *guard of the heart*: Thomas Keating, *Open Mind, Open Heart: The Contemplative Dimension of the Gospel* (New York: Continuum, 1997), pp. 98-99.

p. 162   "I discovered in that moment that I had the power to choose": Gerald L. Sittser, *A Grace Disguised: How the Soul Grows Through Loss* (Grand Rapids: Zondervan, 1996), pp. 33-34.

Chapter 8: Lighting the Lamps

p. 163   "Vespers is the hour that invites peace of heart": David Steindl-Rast, *Music of Silence: A Sacred Journey Through the Hours of the Day* (Berkeley, Calif.: Seastone, 1998), pp. 94-96.

p. 167   "She who reconciles the ill-matched threads of her life": Rainer Maria Rilke, quoted in *Rilke's Book of Hours: Love Poems to God*, trans. Anita Barrows and Joanna Macy (New York: Riverhead, 1996), p. 64.

p. 167   "Then you, God, are the guest": Rilke, quoted in Steindl-Rast, *Music of Silence*, p. 96.

p. 169   "I give Thee thanks, O Lord": Alexander Whyte, *Lord, Teach Us to Pray* (Vancouver, B.C.: Regent College Publishing, 1998), pp. 223-24.

pp. 170-71   Leif Enger's captivating novel: Leif Enger, *Peace like a River* (New York: Atlantic Monthly Press, 2001), pp. 300-304.

pp. 171-72   The story of Sandy's death is told more fully in Leighton Ford, *Sandy: A Heart for God* (Downers Grove, Ill.: InterVarsity Press, 1985), p. 179.

p. 172   "Sensing that we are incomplete": Ronald Rolheiser, *The Holy Longing: The Search for a Christian Spirituality* (New York: Doubleday, 1999), p. 194.

p. 175   "Run madly, as if Time were there": May Sarton, "Now I Become Myself," in *Selected Poems of May Sarton* (New York: W. W. Norton, 1978), p. 191.

p. 176   we spend the first part of our lives finding our role: Thomas Keating, *The Human Condition* (New York: Paulist, 1999), pp. 35.

p. 176   "the beauty of repose": A phrase used by Linda Gregerson to describe the beauty of Jane Kenyon's poetry. In "Review of *The Boat of Quiet Hours* by Jane Kenyon," *Poetry* 151, no. 5 (February 1988): 421.

p. 179   "Centering prayer is not so much an exercise of attention": Thomas Keating, *Open Mind, Open Heart: The Contemplative Dimension of the Gospel* (New York: Continuum, 1997), pp. 36, 39.

p. 180   "I was conscious of being in the company of a world-class contemplative": Parker Palmer, quoted in Michael Ford, *Wounded Prophet* (New York: Doubleday, 1999), p. 5.

p. 180   "To wait for moments or places where no pain exists": Henri Nouwen, *Reaching Out* (New York: Doubleday, 1975), p. 19.

p. 181   "my personal painting": Henri Nouwen, *The Return of the Prodigal Son* (New York: Doubleday, 1992), p. 15.

p. 181   the painting became "a mysterious window": Ibid., pp. 16-17.

Chapter 9: Grandfather Time

p. 183   "Compline completes the circle of the day": David Steindl-Rast, *Music of Silence: A Sacred Journey Through the Hours of the Day* (Berkeley, Calif.: Seastone, 1998), pp. 104-5.

p. 184   "I live my life in widening circles": Rainer Marie Rilke, quoted in *Rilke's Book of Hours: Love Poems to God* trans. Anita Barrows and Joanna Macy(New York: Riverhead, 1996), p. 48.

p. 185   "The new road is not marked at all": Mary C. Morrison, *Let Evening Come: Reflections on Aging* (New York: Doubleday, 1998), p. 16.

p. 185   "Every time I write persuasively": Ibid., p. 119.

p. 187   all times "are contained in something bigger": Cynthia Bourgeault, *Mystical Hope: Trusting in the Mercy of God* (Cambridge, Mass.: Cowley, 2001), pp. 63-64.

p. 190   "turn from our long life of attending to others": Morrison, *Let Evening Come*, pp. 58, 83.

p. 190   T. S. Eliot used the word *end* in "East Coker" and "Little Gidding," in *Four Quartets* (San Diego: Harcourt Brace, 1943), pp. 13, 23, 58.

p. 192   "mysteries are not problems to be solved": Philip Toynbee, *Part of a Journey: An Autobiographical Journal* (London: Fount Paperback, 1981), p. 8.

p. 193   "True and substantial wisdom": John Calvin, *The Institutes of the Christian Religion*, trans. John Allen (Grand Rapids: Eerdmans, 1949), p. 47.

pp. 193-94   "As Kingfishers Catch Fire": Gerard Manley Hopkins, "As Kingfishers Catch Fire" (1918), <www.bartleby.com/122/34.html>, accessed May 31, 2007.

p. 197   *Sleeping with Bread:* Dennis Linn, Sheila Fabricant Linn and Matthew Linn, *Sleeping with Bread: Holding What Gives You Life* (Mahwah, N.J.: Paulist, 1995).

pp. 198-99   Hwee Hwee Tan tells his story in "In Search of the Lotus Land," *Image* 30 (2001): 88-90.

Epilogue

p. 201   "We shall not cease from exploration": T. S. Eliot, "Little Gidding," *Four Quartets* (New York: Harcourt and Brace, 1943), p. 59.

p. 201   "children in the apple tree": T. S. Eliot, "Burnt Norton," *Four Quartets* (New York: Harcourt and Brace, 1943), p. 14.

p. 202   "Now there is time, and Time is young": May Sarton, "Now I Become Myself," in *Selected Poems of May Sarton* (New York: Norton, 1978), p. 191.

In Attention to Gratitude

As this book concludes I sense a leap of gratefulness. My first heart-full thanks is to God, who was paying attention to me long before I was born and has kept watch on my life through these many years, even when I was not paying close enough attention to him.

My second appreciation must go to my family. Our son-in-law Craig and I were having lunch when he asked what I was writing about.

"On attentiveness," I told him.

"Why?" he asked.

"Because our world is so cluttered and busy that it's not easy paying attention," I said. "But the main reason is that I need to learn to pay attention. You know my reputation in the family for getting distracted. In the middle of dinner I would think of something I needed to do and get up and disappear, and the kids would ask, 'What happened to Dad? Where did he go?'"

Jeanie and our children took (and take) my inattentiveness with affectionate humor, and also deserve my full attention. They have been the chief laboratory for practicing it.

For a number of years I sensed a need to write again but had so many ideas that I found it difficult to choose a theme. Then attentiveness chose me.

Many centered my attention on attentiveness as a crucial spiritual pathway: writers like Henri Nouwen, who let us listen in on his conversations with his own soul; poets like Mary Oliver, who confessed that while she did not know too much about prayer, she did know how to pay attention. My first painting instructor, Nancy Oppenheimer-Smolen, taught me that painting is first of all a matter of learning to see, to pay attention to what is actually there.

When the editor of the Wheaton College alumni magazine asked for a reflective piece, I wrote about "coming to attention." An editor from another publication suggested that I write more about it.

Then I was introduced to Kathy Helmers, who has become my agent, sometimes muse, and friend. Kathy helped me to sift through a great mass of jottings and ideas and essays and to focus on some things worth writing about.

Cindy Bunch has been my editor, and a very attentive one. Others told me how good she is at helping authors to keep their own "voice" but also a very good writing coach. They were right. I like Cindy's good humor and perceptive eye and mind. She had a nice way of hinting that I use too many exclamation marks. Actually, without telling me she removed them all from my first draft. Two more are included for you, Cindy!!

For the last twenty years I have been enriched by regular encounters with men and women who have been part of my mentoring groups of younger leaders. On our annual retreats they engaged with me in long and deep conversations about how hard it is (and how important) for those in busy vocations to keep in tune with the movings of the Spirit in their hearts.

So many friends and associates have helped me to shape these ideas. MaryKate Morse and Jim Osterhaus and Anne Grizzle have been coleaders with me in our spiritual mentoring. Elizabeth Richardson commented on some early drafts, shared readings and ideas, and introduced me to Wrangler, my writing companion dog, who is asleep near me as I write this.

David Valtiera, a special spiritual companion on my journey, has helped me to pay attention. He listens carefully and speaks wisely into my life when we meet together at the Oratory in Rock Hill, South Carolina.

Other friends have helped to write this book, paying attention through hospitality. Fred and Ruth Smith let me stay many summers in their highrise above Vancouver's Stanley Park. (And Ruth's painting books inspired me to find my own artistic attentiveness.) Joe and Jane Long hang a key outside their lake house north of Charlotte and tell me to come anytime. Many thoughts in this book have first surfaced in these "away" places.

A special thanks must go to the dedicated members of our Leighton Ford Ministries Board in the United States and Canada. They have been the most enthusiastic supporters of my own "second journey" of ministry, encouraging me in attentive writing, mentoring and teaching.

A final question comes to mind. Have I learned to pay attention more to God, my own heart, others and the world around while writing? I think so. But I probably should ask Craig to call a family meeting to ask whether they have noticed any improvement! I do hope so. And pray so.

Leighton Ford,
Charlotte, North Carolina
November 2007

Permissions

formatio

TRADITION. EXPERIENCE.
TRANSFORMATION.

Formatio books from InterVarsity Press follow the rich tradition of the church in the journey of spiritual formation. These books are not merely about being informed, but about being transformed by Christ and conformed to his image. Formatio stands in InterVarsity Press's evangelical publishing tradition by integrating God's Word with spiritual practice and by prompting readers to move from inward change to outward witness. InterVarsity Press uses the chambered nautilus for Formatio, a symbol of spiritual formation because of its continual spiral journey outward as it moves from its center. We believe that each of us is made with a deep desire to be in God's presence. Formatio books help us to fulfill our deepest desires and to become our true selves in light of God's grace.